5431

D1206545

129

The Theory of Preaching

THE THEORY OF PREACHING
by Dr. Austin Phelps

Abridged and Revised by
Faris Daniel Whitesell, Th.D.

Set up and printed, June, 1947

The Theory of Preaching

by

Dr. Austin Phelps

Abridged and Revised by

Faris Daniel Whitesell, Th.D.

*Professor of Homiletics, Evangelism and Pastoral Theology
in Northern Baptist Theological Seminary,
Chicago, Ill.*

WM. B. EERDMANS PUBLISHING COMPANY

Grand Rapids   1947   Michigan

Preface

Much modern preaching is structurally and logically defective. This defect seriously mars the effectiveness of any sermon, no matter how sound and important its contents may be, and no matter how passionately it may be delivered. No teacher of homiletics ever made a more valuable contribution concerning logical sermonic organization than Dr. Austin Phelps (1820-1890), for over thirty years professor of homiletics at Andover Theological Seminary. His book on *The Theory of Preaching* was published in 1881 and went through many printings. The chief emphases of this book are on exact, logical sermonic structure; sound, good taste; and careful, discriminating style. Dr. Phelps believed that every sermon should have a clean-cut, definitely announced, proposition, followed by logical main divisions firmly rooted in the proposition.

If Dr. Phelps over-emphasized and exaggerated these aspects of sermonic construction, as some authorities say, then it is just as true that we under-emphasize them today. If any preacher can grasp and put into practice Dr. Phelps' teachings regarding sermonic structure, his preaching will be a delight to himself and to his people. His power as a sermonizer is assured.

The Theory of Preaching has been out of print some years, and is available to present-day theological students and ministers only through libraries or second-hand book stores. I have attempted to abridge and revise this valuable homiletical treatise in such a way that its good work can go on. In the original form this book contains 588 pages. This material I have reduced to the first eight chapters of this book. All antiquated illustrations, repetitious material, and extraneous matter have been eliminated, but all the essential homiletic teachings have been retained in the language of the author; revision has been very slight. The ninth chapter of this book is a careful but close abridgement of Dr. Phelps' book, *English Style in Public Discourse*, originally a book of 389 pages, published by Scribner's of New York in 1883. The Appendix contains an outline of Dr. Phelps' book, *Men and Books*, also published by Scribner's as a book of some 250 pages. Some of Dr. Phelps' sermons in outline form and a sketch of his life complete the appendices.

My prayer and hope is that the good work of this great man, as represented herein, may guide and bless this and future generations of preachers of the glorious Gospel of our blessed Lord and Saviour.

FARIS DANIEL WHITESELL.

Chicago, Illinois.

Contents

✓*Chapter 1.* THE SERMON.. 11

    A. The Sermon Defined

        1. An oral address
        2. To popular mind
        3. Upon religious truth
        4. As contained in the Christian Scriptures
        5. Elaborately treated
        6. With a view to persuasion

    B. Sermons Classified

    C. The Parts of a Sermon

Chapter II. THE TEXT.. 19

    A. Positive Uses of Texts

        1. To give authority
        2. To give knowledge of the Bible
        3. To give attachment to Bible language
        4. To facilitate memory
        5. To aid in introducing subject
        6. To promote variety
        7. To preserve unity

    B. Principles for Selecting Texts

        1. The sources of texts
        2. The form of texts
        2. The impression of texts on audience
        4. The relation of texts to main body of sermon
        5. Miscellaneous suggestions

Chapter III. THE EXPLANATION.................................. 36

    A. Explanation Defined

    B. The Objects of Explanation

        1. Verbal criticism
        2. Logical adjustment
        3. Rhetorical amplification

C. The Materials of Explanation

    1. Text itself
    2. Immediate context
    3. Scope of whole argument
    4. Historical and biographical literature
    5. Parallel passages
    6. Common sense in exegesis

D. The Qualities of Explanation

    1. Give true meaning of text
    2. Develop meaning in full force
    3. Do not give more than full force
    4. Make explanation clear
    5. Express positive opinions
    6. Maintain unity of exposition
    7. Make explanation concise
    8. Preserve dignity
    9. Make it interesting
    10. Avoid scholastic weaknesses
    11. Suggest the proposition
    12. Bring text to bear upon conclusion
    13. Vary explanations

E. The Location of the Explanation

Chapter IV. THE INTRODUCTION.................................. 45

A. Introduction Defined

B. Specific Objectives of the Introduction

    1. To secure good-will
    2. To stimulate attention
    3. To secure favorable reception of message

C. The Most Important Characteristic of a Good
   Introduction

    1. Simplicity
    2. Unity
    3. Directness
    4. Congruity
    5. Modesty
    6. Suggestiveness

D. Varieties of Approach
  1. Without an introduction
  2. Introduction applicatory of text
  3. Introduction intensive of text
  4. Introduction explanatory of principles
  5. Introduction narrating facts
  6. Introduction illustrative of facts or principles
  7. Introduction commendary of subject
  8. Introduction connective with preceding messages
  9. Introduction reviewing another subject
  10. Introduction requesting attention

E. Composing the Introduction
  1. Define object
  2. Review growth of subject
  3. Keep whole discourse in view
  4. Outline whole discourse first
  5. Do it with enthusiasm

Chapter V. THE PROPOSITION 56

A. The Proposition Defined

B. The Necessity of a Proposition
  1. Oratorical instinct of good speaker demands it
  2. Instinct of good hearing demands it
  3. Nature of spoken address needs it
  4. Popular mind depends on it
  5. Pulpit subjects need it to avoid confusion
  6. Effectiveness in preaching related to it
  7. Good definition requires it
  8. Used in other fields of presentation

C. May the Proposition Ever Be Omitted
  1. Some apparent exceptions not real ones
  2. Do not conceal aim of sermon

D. Principles Regulating the Substance of a Proposition
  1. Unity
  2. Congruity
  3. Identity

E. The Forms of Propositions
  1. Fundamental distinctions of form
  2. Principles Regulating Forms

Chapter VI. THE DIVISIONS... 76

    A. The Necessity for Divisions

    B. The Extent of Divisions

    C. Abuses of Divisions

    D. Materials of Divisions

    E. The Form of Statement of Divisions

    F. The Order of Divisions

    G. The Mode of Announcing Divisions

Chapter VII. THE DEVELOPMENT................................. 93

    A. Definition of Development

    B. The Foundation of Good Development

        1. The right quantity and quality of materials
        2. The right kind of treatment
        3. Mental dexterity acquired through practice

    C. The Chief Characteristics of Good Development
        1. Unity
        2. Pertinency
        3. Completeness
        4. Conciseness
        5. Order
        6. Proportion

Chapter VIII. THE CONCLUSION.......................................103

    A. The Function of the Conclusion

    B. Causes of Weakness in Conclusions

        1. Lack of spiritual consecration
        2. Overemphasis on the intellectual
        3. Fear of fanaticism
        4. Impractical theological views

    C. The Necessity for Intensity in the Applicatory Uses of Truth

        1. The extreme need of men
        2. The sufficiency of the Gospel
        3. The practicable business of saving men
        4. Supremacy of preaching in saving men
        5. Accordance of preaching with laws of mind

D. Should Applications Ever Be Omitted?

E. Should Applications Run Through the Whole Sermon or All Come at Close?

F. The Fundamental Elements of a Conclusion

G. How to Select and Combine Recapitulation, Appeal, Inference, Remark
   1. On basis of congruity of conclusion with discussion
   2. On basis of progress of moral impression
   3. On basis of variety

H. Qualities Requisite to a Good Recapitulation
   1. Brevity
   2. Restriction
   3. Perspicuity
   4. Climactic order
   5. Variation
   6. Good memorization

I. Qualities Requisite to Construction and Development of the Inference and Remark
   1. Legitimate sequences
   2. Forcible deduction
   3. Unnecessary formality of statement
   4. Use interesting materials
   5. Avoid fantastic materials

J. How Appeals Should Be Conducted
   1. Found on strongest material
   2. Aim at feelings
   3. Aim ultimately at the will
   4. Point toward vital duties
   5. Make them specific
   6. Not unnaturally passionate nor weakly pathetic
   7. Imply expectation of success
   8. Use a natural delivery
   9. Back up by genuine feeling
   10. Keep them brief
   11. Use versatility
   12. Give without forewarning

Chapter IX. STYLE..119

   A. Purity

      1. Definition
      2. Standard Determined
      3. Restriction
      4. Violation of Purity of Style
      5. Reasons for Cultivating Purity of Style
      6. How to Acquire a Pure Style

   B. Precision

      1. Violations of precision
      2. Causes of formation of a loose style
      3. Inducements to cultivation of precision

   C. Perspicuity

      1. Causes of obscurity
      2. Reasons for obscurity
      3. Obscurity due to words
      4. Obscurity due to construction

   D. Energy

      1. Requisites to energy
      2. How to promote energy
      3. Aids to energy

   E. Elegance

      1. Delicacy
      2. Vividness
      3. Variety
      4. Harmony

   F. Naturalness

      1. Forms of naturalness
      2. How to acquire naturalness

APPENDICES

Appendix I. Men and Books..145

Appendix II. Sermon Outlines..................................153

Appendix III. Biographical Sketch of Austin Phelps.........164

Chapter I

THE SERMON

Homiletics is the science which treats of the nature, the classification, the analysis, the construction, and the composition of a sermon. It is the science of which preaching is the art, and a sermon is the product.

A. The Sermon Defined

A sermon is an oral address to the popular mind upon religious truth contained in the Scriptures, and elaborately treated with a view to persuasion.

1. *A sermon is an oral address.* It is distinct from an essay or a book. For perfect public speech the extemporaneous ideal is the true one. A perfect orator would never write, but would always speak. The mutual magnetism between speaker and hearer would bear him on without the aid of manuscript or notes. The custom of preaching written discourses grows out of mental infirmities.

2. *A sermon is an oral address to the popular mind.* It is distinct from the scientific lecture, the judicial oration, the harangue to a rabble, or the talk to children. The best test of a good sermon is the instinct of a heterogeneous audience. The pulpit exists not for the few, not for the many as distinct from the few, but for all. No other form of public speech is so cosmopolitan in its freedom from provincial limitations

as that of the pulpit. The superiority of a sermon considered as a specimen of literature alone is that it sways minds without distinction of class; and in this respect it is the grandest thing in literature.

If a man is swaying a promiscuous assembly every week, even though they have waxed and grimy hands; if he is really moving them, educating them, raising them by the eternal thoughts of God up to the level of those thoughts, he is doing a grander literary work, with more power at both ends of it, than if he were penned in and held down to the elite of a city, or the clique of a university. Follow the literary taste of Christ. Could you conceive of Christ laboring under the burden of literary enthusiasm to improve and polish the Sermon on the Mount, or the Beatitudes, or the Lord's Prayer, and adapting them more tastefully to the upper classes of Judea? Let this mind be in you which was also in Christ Jesus.

3. *A sermon is an oral address to the popular mind upon religious truth.* This quality distinguishes a sermon from secular lectures. They may be popularized and orally delivered but lack the religious theme. Nothing is a sermon which is out of the range of the religious necessities of the people. Usefulness of discourse does not make preaching.

4. *A sermon is an oral address to the popular mind upon religious truth as contained in the Christian Scriptures.* Truth is contained in the Bible by expression and implication. In either mode it has biblical sanction. Inspiration recognizes sources of religious knowledge outside of itself. A sermon, therefore, may follow the line of biblical recognition as well as that of the inspired record. A special significance appertains to this alliance of the sermon in every form and theme of it with the word of God.

The identity of a sermon with scriptural types of thought is emphasized by the fact that preaching owes its existence to revealed religion. It is a remarkable fact that the religion of nature isolated from the Scriptures has never been preached on any large scale. Preaching is both theoretically and historically Christian. It owes its existence to the Christian Scriptures; and nothing but the spirit of biblical religion keeps it alive. Retrograde tendencies in the Christian church from its primeval purity are always tendencies to the disuse of preaching; and revivals of religion go hand in hand with a deepened reverence for the Scriptures and multiplied use of the pulpit.

5. *A sermon is an oral address to the popular mind upon religious truth as contained in the Scriptures, and elaborately treated.* A religious exhortation is not a sermon, nor are informal remarks in a meeting a sermon. Both may be woven into a sermon, but isolated they are not preaching. A sermon is a structure put together with care. It has unity, coherence, proportion, a beginning, a middle, and an end. Some times spontaneous preaching seems to contradict this position. But when we analyze spontaneous preaching we find that it draws upon and utilizes the life-long meditation, reflection, and experience of the preacher. Years of culture are behind it. It is the ripened fruit of thoughts which struggled into the mind years before and have been mellowing there ever since, thoughts which have grown rich in the mind of the preacher through his own long experience of them in his own character. Rest assured that spontaneous preaching is truly useful just in proportion to its cost in previous labor. Up to the extreme border of your own hard bought experience, you can preach thus with power, but beyond that border such preaching is the weakest of all possible dilutions. When it ceases

to be an experience, and becomes an imitation, it wins no hearts, because it commands no respect. The sermon must be a structure, and therefore the fruit of elaboration.

6. *A sermon is an oral address to the popular mind upon religious truth contained in the Scriptures, and elaborately treated with a view to persuasion.* The immediate object of a sermon may be instruction, or the excitement of emotion, or both; but the ultimate object is always the persuasion of the hearer. This persuasive intention is to preaching what the circulation of the blood is to the vital powers of the body. If it languishes, life languishes, and when it ceases, life goes out.

B. Classification of Sermons

Sermons may be classified upon various principles. One is the mode of delivery, whether delivered from manuscript, from memory, or extemporaneously. Another classification is founded upon the subjects of sermons, such as doctrinal, practical, historical, ethical, and philosophical. A useful classification is that based upon the way the Scriptures are handled in the sermon—the topical, the textual, the expository, and the inferential. See Appendix II for examples. The topical sermon is one in which a subject is deduced from the text, but discussed independently of the text. The textual sermon is one in which the text is the theme, and the parts of the text are the divisions of the discourse, and are used as a line of suggestion. An expository sermon is one in which the text is the theme, and the discussion is an explanation of the text. The inferential sermon is one in which the text is the theme, and the discussion is a series of inferences directly from the text.

Let me illustrate these four classes of sermons by example from the same text, Phil. 2:12-13,

> "Work out your own salvation with fear and trembling; for it is God which worketh in you both to will and to do of his good pleasure."

From this text we might deduce the subject of the "Sovereignty of God in the Work of Salvation," or the subject of the "Activity of Man in Regeneration," or the "Duty of Earnestness in Seeking Salvation." Either of these subjects might then be discussed independently of any further use of the text, and we should thus have a topical sermon.

But we might make the text itself the theme of the discourse and follow its line of thought by remarking:

1. The duty taught in the text, *"Work out* your own salvation;"

2. The individual responsibility for the soul's salvation implied in the text, "Work out *your own* salvation;"

3. The spirit with which salvation should be sought, "With fear and trembling;"

4. The dependence of effort to be saved upon the power of God, "It is God which worketh in you;"

5. Dependence upon God for salvation is the great encouragement to effort for salvation, "Work, for it is God which worketh in you."

This train of thought developed would constitute a textual sermon.

Yet again we might make the text the theme, and let the sermon consist of an explanation of the text, by inquiring:

1. In what sense is a sinner commanded to achieve his own salvation?

2. What is the spirit of fear and trembling in the work of salvation?

3. In what sense does the text affirm God to be the author of salvation?

4. What connection does the text affirm between the earnestness of the sinner and the agency of God?

An answer to these inquiries, devoted to the language of the text, and designed to evolve the force of the text, would constitute an expository sermon. The complete expository sermon, however, contains more than explanation of the text. It contains all of the other rhetorical processes necessary to its perfection—narration, illustration, application, argumentation, and exhortation.

Once more, we might consider the text as the theme, and assume that, as a well-known passage, it does not need much explanation. Explain it briefly, if you wish, give in a paraphrase the result without the process of exposition, and let the body of the sermon consist of a series of inferences drawn directly from the text.

1. That salvation is a pressing necessity to every man.

2. That every man is responsible for his own salvation.

3. That every man who is saved does in fact achieve his own salvation.

4. That dependence upon God is a help, not a hindrance, to salvation.

5. The guilt of trifling with religious convictions.

6. The unreasonableness of waiting in impenitence for the interposition of God.

7. The uselessness of lukewarm exertions to secure salvation.

8. The certainty that every man who is in earnest to be saved will be saved.

This line of thought developed would be an inferential sermon. Its characteristic feature is neither topical, nor textual, nor expository discussion, but independent yet direct inferences from the text.

A fourth method of classification of sermons is founded on the mode of treating the subject of discourse. By this principle, sermons may be arranged in four classes, namely, the explanatory, the illustrative, the argumentative, and the persuasive. Explanatory sermons include all sermons the chief object of which is explanation, whether it be a text, a doctrine, or a duty. Illustrative sermons seek to intensify the vividness of truth, not so much to formulate or explain truth, but to impart glow to it. This includes historical and biographical sermons in which pictorial imaginaton holds the place of preeminence. Argumentative sermons are those in which the chief object is proof. They are aimed primarily at the intellect of the hearer, and the prime element is logic pure and simple. All sermons should be persuasive, and nothing is truly a sermon which is not aimed at persuasion, but we classify as persuasive sermons those whose immediate object is persuasion. The key-note of the persuasive sermon is urgency to present action.

The proper classification of sermons is fundamental to the subject of unity of discourse. A sermon cannot be pointed in its aim, if it has no oneness of rhetorical character by which to classify it. The same qualities which adjust it to its class give it unity as an individual. Also, the proper classification of sermons is equally fundamental to the subject of proportion in preaching. The preacher should seek for variety in the types of sermons he preaches. No variety of subject, of text, of occasion, of audience, will save you from monotony, if you always do one and the same thing with subject, text, occasion, and audience. Construct your sermons for ten years so that you have symmetrical proportions of argumentative, of illustrative, of explanatory, and of persuasive materials, and you have symmetry of impression, without the possibility of monotony or of distortion.

C. Parts of a Sermon

The constituent parts of a sermon are* the text, the explanation, the introduction, the proposition, the divisions, the development, and the conclusion. The material composing the next eight chapters will be a discussion of these seven principal parts of a sermon.

------.

*Dr. Phelps does not give the subject, or topic, as one of the principal parts of a sermon. Most modern books on homiletics treat the subject as an important part of the sermon. This is doubtless due to the large use of subjects for newspaper announcements, bulletin-board notices, and church bulletin orders of service. Dr. Phelps sometimes uses the word "theme" as practically identical with the subject, or topic; but other times he uses the same word as meaning the proposition.

CHAPTER II

THE TEXT

THE Bible as a whole and in all its parts is the Word of God and must ever be the source book for Christian preaching. A scholarly care for verbal exposition of an inspired book is not pedantry. An inspired production deserves a minuteness of exegesis of which no other production is worthy. The words of the Scriptures are to the popular mind like the words of a will by which an inheritance is conveyed —every word is important and may be emphatic.

For the first twelve centuries of the Christian era, the restriction of the text to an isolated verse, or fragment of a verse, of the Bible was unknown. The topical sermon was an innovation. Originally the Christian sermon was an exposition, and only that. The restriction of the text to a verse, or a fragment of a verse, met with strenuous opposition for two hundred years. It originated about 1200 A.D. and the older clergy of that day contested it stoutly.

The modern period in the history of the custom of employing texts dates from the Reformation. At that time, there was a return to the ancient usage respecting the sources of texts. The religious vitality of the Reformation is indicated in no other way so signally as in this backward spring from human to inspired authorities in the search for a preacher's texts. There was a similar return to the ancient simplicity in the interpretation of texts, namely, on the same principles of grammatico-historical exegesis by which common sense interprets the language of any other ancient volume. A third feature which the Reformation period gave us is a variety of usage respecting the objects for which texts are employed.

A. Positive Uses of Texts

There are advantages in using texts, and objects to be aimed at in the selection of texts. We will consider both together. That is the best text which secures the largest number and the most vital of the objects of having a text.

1. *A text gives inspired authority to the sentiments of a sermon.* This is its prime object. If the Bible be an inspired volume, it is inspired for a purpose. If inspired for a purpose, it is divinely fitted to that purpose. If fitted to that purpose, it is a compend of the truths most necessary to the world in all time. Distinctions of past, present, and future do not destroy its pertinence as a whole. It can contain nothing which for the purposes of such a volume can ever be obsolete. The world will always need it, and will need the whole of it. As a unit, it will be as fresh to the last man as to you and to me.

A text as an inspired authority is of special value in the preaching of unpopular doctrines. On the doctrine of future punishment, for example, it is not the argumentations of the pulpit which hold the popular mind to the truth most rigidly: it is the downright and inevitable authority of a few texts.

This use of texts encourages a regulated freedom in the pulpit, and is no hindrance to such freedom. Some subjects, it is true, are not expressed in any scriptural text; but, if they are not expressed, they may be contained in a principle which is expressed. Some principles, it is true, are not affirmed in a declarative form; but they may be implied in a narrative, a parable, an act, a character which is recorded. If a subject is not expressed in any scriptural passage, and is not contained in any scriptural principle, and is not implied in any scriptural narrative, parable, event, or character, and is not, by any manly association of thought suggested by any scriptural language, then it is doubtful if the Christian preacher should waste time discussing it.

This practice tends to put a preacher in his true relation to divine authority. The real character of a preacher as a minister of God, speaking for God, uttering God's thoughts, is silently kept before his own mind and that of his hearers. The tendency is to impart a most vitalizing spiritual influence to both—to him in giving; to them in receiving.

2. *The use of texts promotes popular intelligence in the perusal of the Scriptures.* It is no small benefit to a people to hear a hundred passages of the Bible expounded accurately and practically every year. Popular knowledge of the Bible and Christianity is largely dependent upon the preaching the people hear. Exposition of texts is the exposition of the choicest passages of the Bible. Well-chosen texts are the gems of scriptural thought. They represent fundamental doctrines, vital principles, essential duties, central characters, critical events, thrilling scenes, and profound experiences. They are the dense points of revelation at which light is most vivid. The Bible is dotted with them. To see them is to see the whole firmament of truth in which they are set. They are constellations in a cloudless sky. An intelligent and scholarly explanation of a thousand texts might indoctrinate people in the whole system of biblical truth.

3. *Again, the use of texts tends to cherish in the minds of hearers an attachment to the language of the Bible.* Words very easily become things. Never is language more readily consolidated into a living thing around which the reverence

of a people will grow than when that language is long used to express their religious conviction, or their religious inheritance from their fathers. Therefore, if reverence is not cherished for the scriptural forms of truth, it will be for uninspired forms. It is impossible to express some forms of truth more concisely and exactly than in the very words of scripture.

4. *Usage of a text facilitates a hearer's remembrance of the truths presented.* The best texts are brief statements of truth. They are easily remembered, and yet they contain a comprehensive view of the whole scope of the sermon founded upon them. The most felicitously chosen texts are the sermons in miniature. The sermons are in them like an oak in the acorn. To recall them is to recall the train of thought which the sermons develop. Further: inspired language, other things being equal, impresses the memory the more strongly for being inspired. It is authoritative language. Memory is assisted by reverence for authority. Inspired language is usually of uncommon raciness. The Bible is the most brilliant book in the world as to style. It abounds in sententious utterances of truth. It is a book of axioms. Its imagery is fascinating. Its style pulsates with life. It has a wonderful power to fasten itself in the human memory.

5. *A text aids in the introduction of a subject of discourse.* As a preventive against sameness, texts offer the preacher an almost infinite variety of approaches to the basic truths of life. And since the preacher has no time for leisurely, circumlocutory approach to his theme, a text will facilitate brevity of preliminaries. Often a text is the subject. When it is not such, it may suggest material for an explanatory approach to the subject. When it needs no explanation, it

may suggest the best material for an introduction proper. Remarks not explanatory of the text, and yet suggested directly by the text may lead to the theme quickly and in a way which shall stimulate attention. Some times a text itself may be such as to awaken interest in a subject.

6. *The use of texts promotes variety in preaching.* The Bible is full of diversified original forms of truth. It contains every variety of style known to literature. If the prime object of the biblical revelation had been to prepare a book of texts for the pulpit, a more copious variety of fresh thought could hardly have been collected in any other form. Let a preacher stamp upon his ministry the biblical impress by representative texts unfolded by sermons which are true to their texts, and he has an absolute guaranty of a symmetrical pulpit.

Inspired thought often presents in a single text original combinations of truth. Pure intellect and pure emotion play in and out, often, in the structure of a text, with the artlessness yet without the incoherence of dreams.

The usage of preaching from texts promotes versatility of habit in a preacher's mental culture. If mind grows by what it feeds upon, a preacher's mind can not habituate itself to thinking in scriptural lines of suggestion without acquiring some degree of scriptural versatility in its own lines of thought.

7. *Texts aid in the preservation of unity in sermons.* It is true that many texts appear to be heterogeneous in material: they are not a single thesis. But, on the other hand, the large majority of texts are logically one in their structure. They invite a strictly synthetic discourse. If a paragraph of a chapter does not, a single verse may: if a verse does not, a portion of it may. It is optional with the preacher to

select more or less of the inspired record. Intensity of aim
is characteristic of inspired thought. Intensity of aim is
singleness of aim. An eager mind thinks in right lines: so
an inspired mind thinks with a vigorous tension of intellect
and always for an object. Rambling thought is the work of
an idle mind. The Scriptures have none of it. Hence paragraphs of inspired thought often develop the point of unity
when a verse does not. A chapter may develop the point of
unity when a paragraph may seem to have none. Fidelity to
the spirit of texts in preaching, then, will secure unity of
aim through the force of the sympathy of a preacher's mind
with the intensity of inspired thinking and feeling. Any
collection of inspired words which have neither rhetorical
nor logical unity is not a text. Sermons true to texts will
have as real a unity as sermons on a logical thesis.

From these considerations, it is obvious that the selection
of texts is of vast moment to the work of the pulpit. It is to
the pulpit what the work of adjusting the range of guns is
to a battery. The study of texts essential to intelligent
selection is one of the most healthful moral preparations to
a preacher's mind for the work of constructing a sermon.
Preachers of earnest piety are more frequently sensible of
intuitions which seem to them to be direct from the Holy
Ghost in their selection of texts than in any other portion
of their preparation for the pulpit.

B. Inquiries Concerning the Principles of Selection of Texts

Since the business of selection of texts is so important, it
might seem natural to proceed to lay down rules of selection.
But we experience difficulty if we try to subject ourselves to
rigid rules in a matter like this. I prefer to consider the

principles of selection under the general title of inquiries rather than rules respecting the choice of texts. The most important inquiries respecting the selection of texts group themselves naturally into four classes.

1. *The sources of texts.*

(1) May we select and use as a text an interpolated passage or a mistranslation? The answer is, we should not commonly choose for texts passages which need correction. When we do use such texts, we should correct them, else we injure our own mental and moral habits, and impose upon the faith of an audience. The genuine translation is the Word of God, and nothing different. Cautiously and reverently, but faithfully, we should attach the reverence of the people to the exact Word of God, not to the most useful substitute; to the exact Word of God, not to the interpolations of monks, nor to the wisdom of the King James' translators.

(2) May we select as texts passages the sentiment of which is not inspired? We mean the record in the Bible of the false sayings of wicked beings like Cain, Ahab, Saul, Herod, Judas, and Satan; or the false sentiments of good men, such as the arguments of Job's friends; or the true sentiments of men not inspired, as found in many historical and biographical passages.

These passages constitute a large portion of the Scriptures and are a good source of texts. They are in the Bible by inspiration of record, and hold a rank which an interpolation and a mistranslation do not. "Who can forgive sins but God only?" was a truth uttered by men, who, in the same breath, charged our Lord with blasphemy. Many of these uninspired passages are confirmed by others which are inspired. But often times an uninspired passage may have rhetorical advantages over an inspired text of the same sentiment. Words from the lips of a doubting disciple may carry more weight than even inspired words addressed to such a disciple. Many of these texts are valuable specimens of the working of uninspired minds. We should never use such texts as proof-texts of doctrine, and we should not give this source of texts an undue proportion in our sermons. Then we should always discuss the context and explain that they are not from inspired sources.

2. *The form of texts.*

(1) Must the text be a grammatical sentence? The answer is yes, as a general rule. It is dangerous to use fragments of texts, except in cases in which the fragments chosen are very weighty in thought, and so well known that they instantly suggest the complete idea, such as, "Like people, like priest." The thought is racy, and at the same time complete, though the form is not complete. In doubtful cases, the entire passage should be cited with a repetition of the textual fragment.

(2) Can any principle regulate the length of texts? There are good arguments for both long and short texts? Long texts are more in accord with the original theory of the text. They familiarize people with the Bible, and tend to conserve the ancient reverence for the inspired utterances. Long texts promote a taste for exposition among the people, and invite a preacher to expository discourse.

On the other hand, short texts have advantages which should sometimes give them the preference. They are more easily remembered; they promote unity of discourse; every word in the text can be emphasized; no needless exposition is necessary to introduce them; and such texts can be repeated several times in the course of the sermon for emphasis.

Our general rule then is to fit the text to the demands of the subject. The advantages in either direction are only secondary; but the demands of the subject are always imperative. They will necessitate variety.

(3) May we choose for one sermon more than one text? We should generally adopt but one text. We should never choose more than one text without an obvious demand for it in the nature of the theme, or of its discussion. Two or more texts should not be chosen merely for the purpose of dignifying a subject by an accumulation of inspired statements of it. The text is not the place for this. If the subject is one, the text should be one. Neither should two or more texts be announced for the sake of discussing two or more independent subjects in one sermon. No such discussions of independent subjects are permissible in one sermon. The law of unity forbids them. Two or more texts may properly be chosen for a subject which is twofold, or manifold, and for which no single text can be found which covers its whole range. In a sermon designed to reconcile the benevolence with the justice of God, one might announce the double text: "God is love," and "God is a consuming fire."

3. *The impression of texts upon the audience.*

(1) Should a preacher always use perspicuous texts? Clear texts have positive advantages. They immediately suggest the subjects derived from them; they save time, since no explanation of them is needed; they facilitate long and intricate discussions, since the intellectual strength of the audience is saved for the discussion; they assist the illiterate part of an audience to comprehend and recollect the sermon; and another advantage of transparent texts is that they bring biblical authority to the front at the outset of the discussion. For

these reasons some have advised the selection of only transparent texts.

However, there are also some advantages in using obscure texts. Obscure texts need to be explained in order that the people may understand the Scriptures. Such texts often facilitate a gradual approach to the subject of discussion; they may be intriguing and stir up more interest than clear texts; they tend to appeal to the more cultivated hearers; and they help to train the less cultivated hearers to more reflective habits. Negatively, never choose an obscure text unless you can make it plain. Never choose such texts so often that you give the impression that the Bible contains nothing but obscurities. And, the rhetorical effects being equal, never choose an obscure text when a clear text covering the same sentiments is available.

(2) Ought we to select texts of an elevated emotional character? These are sometimes called "promising texts." An example is, "They rest not day and night, saying, Holy, holy, holy, Lord God Almighty, which was, and is, and is to come." The grand text needs to be buoyed up by a grand sermon. Such a text invites a preacher into an impassioned introduction, which is very rarely natural. Then the rest of the sermon should measure up to the introduction. There is danger of bombast in a futile attempt to equal promising texts. Some passages of Scripture no uninspired mind can imitate.

In spite of the real difficulties in the treatment of such texts, yet, on the other hand, they can not always be dispensed with. They form a most significant portion of God's word. Some of the themes of the pulpit are intrinsically grand, awful, overpowering: others are plaintive, beautiful, exquisite. Such subjects need congruous texts. Then some occasions demand eloquent texts. The theme must be great, the sermon great, and the text on a level with both.

Promising texts must be admitted to the pulpit. Yet, as they are liable to abuse, we have occasion to remember certain cautions in the use of them. They should not be the exclusive favorites of a preacher. Eloquent texts, often chosen, degenerate in the popular esteem. We should guard against the dangers incident to the treatment of promising texts. Those dangers, though real, are not inevitable. If a preacher is self-possessed under the inspiration of his text, he will use it: he will not suffer it to use him.

(3) What is essential to the dignity of a text? The dignity of a text requires that it shall not be restricted to a single word standing alone. Word studies wherein the usage and significance of an important word is traced through the whole Bible, or at least through a Bible book, can be profitable; but no text should be mutilated by using single words, or phrases, or clauses, apart from the whole text and context. An apparent exception is where a passage is retrenched by elision, and yet is a pertinent text, because the fragment chosen does not depart from the spirit of the whole. "By grace are ye saved" is a good text, because the fragment, and the passage from which it is taken lie on the same plane and in the same line of thought.

It is essential to the dignity of texts that they should not be such as to suggest low or ludicrous associations. We should not use a text in such a way as to violate modern and occidental ideas of delicacy.

(4) What principles should govern a preacher respecting the choice of novel texts? The pulpit has some standard texts, such as Acts 16:31. They seem as if foreordained primarily for use in discussing certain important themes in the pulpit.

It would be inexcusable to avoid using these standard texts. They are among the jewels of the pulpit. Diamonds are never obsolete.

Yet, on the other hand, a large proportion of sermons should be upon unhackneyed texts. Novel texts are desirable for the sake of the interest they excite. This interest may not be the most profound but it may lead to a more valuable interest. One of the most masterly successes of the pulpit is that of freshening an old story and novel texts aid in doing this. Again, novel texts promote variety in preaching, and will often facilitate permanence of impression. A truth is apt to be deepened in its impression upon us if it comes to us from an unexpected source. Also an unhackneyed text invites effort on the part of a preacher. It stimulates his mind in the composition of a sermon as it does the hearer in listening to the sermon.

Therefore, we conclude that while we recognize some standard texts, yet, other things being equal, an unhackneyed text is preferable.

(5) May a preacher choose texts which to an audience will seem to be personal? A preacher must not in the choice of texts disregard the claims of courtesy. He should not avoid pungency in his texts, yet he should not take texts that point directly at some individual in his audience. We should never wrest Scripture from its own proper sense, and from all good sense, to make it apply to some individual or class of individuals. Modesty is a power in a public man. A genuine modesty will prevent a preacher from thrusting himself immoderately, or in an untimely way, upon the attention of his hearers. Again, a preacher has no right to invade the privacy of domestic life. As a preacher a man may not say

every thing which as a pastor he may say. But a man may say in the body of a sermon what he may not say in a text.

4. *The relation of a text to the main body of the sermon.*

(1) On what principles shall we judge of the pertinency of a text? Pertinency to the sermon is the most vital quality of a good text. The pertinency of a text relates chiefly to congruity of sentiment between text and theme. A perfect text will express exactly the subject of the sermon, no more, and no less. Congruity of sentiment then may be sacrificed in several ways. First, when the text does not contain the subject, either expressly, or by implication, or by natural suggestion. Secondly, when the text contains the subject, but not the proposition; that is, where it contains a different aspect of the subject from that which the sermon discusses. Thirdly, when a general text is chosen for a specific subject. A specific text for a specific theme is not always practicable. Some subjects are not specifically named, or implied, or suggested, in the Scriptures. For such themes we are compelled to choose a general text; that is, an inferior text. Still this quality of pertinency of sentiment is the crowning virtue of a text: it should never be needlessly sacrificed or impaired. Many preachers habitually choose unsuggestive texts.

Pertinency of texts is not restricted to sentiment. It relates also to congruity of rhetorical structure between the text and the sermon. Is there not, to the eye of good taste, an incongruity between a very imaginative text and a severely argumentative discourse? Do we not feel a similar infelicity between a difficult logical text, and a hortatory address? Pertinency of rhetorical structure often is not practicable. We should not subject ourselves to a rule requiring it: still it is a beauty where it is attainable, and very many themes of the pulpit admit of variety of choice in this respect.

Pertinency of texts relates also to congruity of the associations of the text with the object of the sermon. The associations of a text should, if possible, be such as to aid the subject of the sermon. Thus a text may aid a subject by the force of sympathy with it. You wish to preach a sermon on diligence in the Christian life, and you use as a text the words expressive of the youthful awakening of Christ to his life's work, "Wist ye not that I must be about my Father's business?"

(2) What principles apply to the regulation of incompleteness and redundancy in texts? Good taste requires that a text should comprise no less material than is discussed in the sermon. The text should, in some natural development of thought, cover the whole area of a sermon: it should not be a patch upon the fabric. Again, good taste requires that, if possible, a text shall comprise no more material than is discussed in the sermon. This tends to promote unity of impression. Study of texts for the sake of retrenchment down to the precise limits of the subjects is the mark of an accomplished preacher. A text is for use. Enough is better than more. One advantage of deriving subjects from texts, instead of choosing texts for subjects, is that redundancy of text is more easily avoided. But sometimes we cannot find a passage which expresses exactly our theme, no more and no less. We must, then, admit redundancy as a less evil than incompleteness. Too much is a less evil than too little.

Good taste forbids the elimination of superfluous material from within the limits of a text. This error is not that of mutilating a text for the sake of a forced pertinency; nor is it that of elision from the end of a passage, nor that of omission from its beginning: it is elimination from within a text, as superfluous terms are thrown out of an algebraic equation. When a redundant text is necessary, we should repeat all that is needed to avoid elimination, and then specify the words which are the text.

(3) May a preacher employ an accommodated text? An accommodated text is one which is applied in a sermon to a subject resembling that of the text, yet radically different from that of the text. A remote application is not identical with accommodation. One minister used the text from Micah, "Arise ye and depart; for this is not your rest," to teach the doctrine of regeneration. He pointed out that there is in regeneration an arising and a departing from an old state to a new at the command of God. But the text does not express or imply this doctrine. It suggests the doctrine of regeneration only by accommodation.

Accommodated texts may be of three kinds; first, where the resemblance beween text and theme is only in sound; second, where there is only a metaphorical resemblance; and third, where the resemblance is in principle—the principle in the text resembles the principle of the subject, but is radically different from it.

Some will say that we should never use accommodated texts. We should not use accommodated texts on the ground of resemblance, for this is puerile. Manly culture revolts from it. Also, accommodation on the ground of metaphorical resemblance is also to be condemned. Such accommodation is not natural to a well-trained mind when that mind is in earnest. It belongs to a sportive or a fanciful state of mental activity. But, the accommodation of texts on the ground of resemblance in principle between the text and the theme is admissible. When an English king entered the fiftieth year of his reign, one of England's preachers delivered a sermon from a text in Leviticus, "It shall be a jubilee unto you." Here the subject of the text is not the subject of the sermon. The text can not logically be made to cover the sermon; yet there is more than resemblance in sound or figure; there is resemblance in principle. Such accommodation is a natural use of a text.

Our minds are so made that similar principles suggest each other. Also, this is a scriptural use of a text. Passages from the Old Testament are sometimes quoted in the New Testament, as fulfillments of prophecy, on no other principle than this of accommodation. Furthermore, this kind of accommodation is often a pleasing use of a text. So far from detracting from the value of a text, if not abused, it augments that value, through the interest which the mind feels in the discovery of resemblance. Therefore, we accept the usage of accommodation of texts on the ground of resemblance in principle, but reject all accommodation on the ground of resemblance in sound or in metaphor.

(4) May preachers properly employ motto-texts? A motto-text is not necessarily an accommodated text. "The field is the world" may be a motto-text for a sermon on the conversion of India to Christianity, but it can not be accommodated to that subject. The subject is logically related to the text. A motto implies two things, — remoteness of connection between the text and the theme, and independence of the text in the discussion of the theme. Some times a text may be both a motto and an accommodated text.

Motto-texts, like accommodated texts, should not be used as a practice, but some defense can be made for them. The exclusion of such texts would restrict injuriously the range of the topics of the pulpit. Such texts are a necessity to any broad compass of thought in preaching. Some themes of modern times cannot be discussed under a text unless it be by remote relation. It is always better in a Christian pulpit to have a text, even though it be a motto-text, than to have none. Motto-texts are a less evil than a forced intimacy between text and sermon would be. We consider motto-texts a less evil than accommodated texts.

5. *Miscellaneous suggestions regarding texts.*

(1) The text should be located in the place of honor in the sermon. This will usually be at the beginning of the sermon, but may some times be at the end of the introduction.

(2) If texts are not long, they may be repeated when they are announced. Some times emphasis may require repetition; again, elegance may forbid it.

(3) Always introduce texts by giving the book, the chapter, and the verse, never the reverse of this. There is but one natural order to announce the location of the text.

(4) Vary the method of prefacing texts. Cultivate simplicity and variety in this respect. It is a gross violation of simplicity to announce a text with a pompous or long-winded preface.

A keen sense of the reverence due to the Scriptures should be associated with a liberal construction of the rules for selecting texts. That is the best text for a sermon which associates it in the most manly, free, and intimate connection with the Word of God.

Chapter III

THE EXPLANATION

A. Explanation Defined

EXPLANATION is that part of a sermon which comprehends all those remarks of which the object is to adjust the meaning of the text to the homiletic use which is to be made of it. The explanation as a part of a topical sermon concerns exclusively the text and its contemplated uses. It may not be the chief feature of a discourse: it may be the briefest incident to the chief discussion. The explanation as executed should be distinguished from the process of investigation. Explanation is an after process to that of discovery: it concerns the results of investigation, not the process. Explanation often differs from exegesis. Exegesis concerns a text, with no reference to its homiletic uses, but the explanation concerns a text, with no other reference than to its homiletic uses. Its aim is to make the text useful.

The explanation, as a part of a topical or a textual sermon, is distinct from exposition in an expository sermon. The distinction is, that the one is only a preliminary, while the other is the bulk of the sermon. What the explanation in a topical sermon is, that the body of an expository sermon is, with this difference only, that one is preliminary and the other is not.

B. The Objects of Explanation

1. *Verbal criticism.* Verbal criticism may take the form of an analysis of the text. A text sometimes needs to be par-

titioned in order to be appreciated. Significant words need to be distinguished; points of emphasis need to be made obvious; an ellipsis may need to be amplified; a person implied may need to be expressed. Or verbal criticism may be necessary in the form of a verbal paraphrase, or in the form of correction of the text.

2. *Logical adjustment.* The logical relations of the text to the context may need to be adjusted. A text intelligible in itself may seem to contradict the context, or to be irrelevant to the context. If not the truth, at least the force, of a text may depend on certain logical connections with the context, which are not obvious. To make them obvious may be all the exposition which the text demands. The logical relations of the text to other portions of the Scriptures than the context may require adjustment. An explanation achieves much for a sermon if it makes distant Scriptures buttress a text. The relations of a text to arguments confirmatory of its interpretation may require adjustment. The protection of a text from a distorted literalism may depend on matching it well with homely examples of common speech. The relations of a text to certain intuitions of man may need adjustment. One of the first duties of a preacher is to keep inspired language in line with the necessary beliefs of men.

3. *Rhetorical amplification.* Oftener than otherwise, this is the chief object. A text which needs no verbal criticism and no logical adjustment may need to be amplified. Texts are often but hints. An explanation should expand them. Explanation should do the work of a telescope in bringing a distant truth near, and of the microscope in disclosing the beauty of a minute truth. Explanation may be illustrative paraphrase or descriptive incident.

C. The Materials of Explanation

1. *The words of the text itself.* This is obvious.

2. *The immediate context.* This is equally obvious. Popular interest in a text will often depend on a skillful use of the context.

3. *The scope of the whole argument from which a text is taken.* Not merely the text, not merely the immediate context, but the drift of an epistle is often essential to a truthful interpretation of a word. A precept, a doctrine, an ordinance depends, it may be, not on a text, nor on its proximate paragraphs, but on the aim of a volume. The root shows what the branch must be.

4. *The historical and biographical literature of texts.* Facts respecting the character of the writer, events in his history, the places from which he wrote, the time at which he wrote, the immediate occasion of his writing, the place held by him in the biblical canon, the literary qualities of his productions, the character of the persons addressed—these and similar materials you recognize as being often the expository setting in which texts are presented by the pulpit. Everything vitalizes a text, which, in a natural way, introduces persons into and around it. It is a great thing to establish in the popular convictions the pertinence of the Scriptures to modern wants; and very largely this must be done by the apt use of the historical and biographical literature of texts.

5. *The comparison of texts with parallel passages of the Scriptures.* This helps define the limits of an interpretation. Many texts are truths in their extremes. The common mind is childlike in its tendency to literalism and its attachment to inherited beliefs. The most effective method of giving

balanced interpretations is to make Scripture interpret Scripture. Explain a metaphor by a literal passage. Offset one extreme by its opposite in biblical speech. A disputed text expound by parallels which are not disputed.

Parallel passages are useful in explaining peculiarities of idiom. New Testament Hebraisms are often best explained by parallels from the Old Testament. The interpretation of an idiom comes to light of itself, if we can collect examples of it in groups. Parallels are valuable in explanations for purposes of illustration. A text declarative of a principle may be explained by a biblical narrative illustrating the principle. Finally, parallels are valuable in explanations as confirmatory arguments. The exposition is precisely the place in which to strengthen an interpretation by reduplication of it from other texts.

6. *The application of the philosophy of common sense to exegesis.* We bring to the Bible, antecedently to our interpretation of it, the germs of philosophy by which we understand it, if at all. We can not help this. The Bible, rightly interpreted, has an almost omnipotent ally in the common sense of common people: falsely interpreted, it has as potent a foe there.

D. The Qualities of Explanation

1. *It should give the true meaning of a text.* Effective sermons have been preached on inherited misinterpretations of texts, and souls have been saved by such sermons, but let us not follow such a practice. The meaning of the text is the text. A misinterpreted text is no part of the Bible. Many popular misinterpretations are inferior in homiletic value to the true interpretations. A want of accuracy in the explanation of the Scriptures is hazardous to the authority of the

pulpit. The hearers may come to believe that a preacher's interpretations are not trustworthy. Hearers are more shrewd than is often supposed in detecting a real weakness in the pulpit.

2. *It should develop the meaning of the text in its full force.* The signification of a text is one thing; its significance is another. The signification of a text is complete when its words are truthfully interpreted, and its grammatical idea expressed, while its significance is its signification clothed in all that is needful for vividness of impression. Picturesque explanations are especially necessary to the interpretation of an ancient volume like the Bible. It is also a foreign volume to us. We must read the Bible through a foreign atmosphere—language, climate, nationality, customs, politics, sciences, etc. Picturesque explanation is especially necessary to the popular mind. The pulpit must modernize and Americanize texts, and thus fit them to a modern American audience. This power of picturesque invention is the hinge of the whole question of expository preaching. The preacher who has it in any large degree is always a power in the pulpit.

3. *Explanation should not give to a text more than its full force.* Do not invent materials not inherent in the text. Unchastened rhetorical painting may lead to exaggerated explanation. Some men distort the truth of history to make it fit prophecy and thus exaggerate explanation. In handling the parables, there is danger in forcing the details and in digging for the occult sense of words to the exaggeration of the parable.

4. *Explanation should be clear.* An obscure explanation is a self-contradiction. Obscure explanation may be due to unfamiliarity with oriental life and civilization; or to needless use of technical terms; or to confusion of philosophical

distinctions; or to want of naturalness of arrangement; or to shallow study on the part of the preacher.

5. *An explanation should, if possible, express positive opinions.* Hearers have a right to expect defined and settled convictions from one in the pulpit. They do not want dogmatism, but they do demand confidence of judgment. He who believes will be heard in preference to the man who doubts. The Scriptures are the foundation of the pulpit. Texts are its pillars. In exegesis, if in any thing, a preacher needs confident opinions.

6. *Another necessary quality of explanation is unity of exposition.* This is an exceeding subtile quality, and we should try never to sacrifice it. Lack of unity is one of the greatest weaknesses of much so-called expository preaching. We should limit expository preaching to passages of Scripture which clearly have unity of structure, until we can develop ability to find unity in more difficult passages. The Bible is an inexhaustible source of Scripture passages with unity if we look for them. We some times sacrifice unity of explanation by needless dealing with conflicting interpretations, or by irrelevant verbal exposition, or by erroneous representations of the "double sense" of certain passages, or by taking too long a passage.

7. *Explanation should be as concise as clearness and fullness will permit.* Conciseness itself stimulates interest. We should condense. Make every word significant. Say nothing in a rotary way. Let every step be an advance. The temptation to indolent composition is nowhere more insidious than in the explanation. The very nature of the process invites delay. If any doubt exists as to the interest of an audience in an expository discourse, condense; pack your thoughts;

shorten the process; make haste; come quickly to the gist of things; and you are sure of one element of success. Conciseness of explanation may be sacrificed by explaining things which need no explanation, or by dwelling needlessly upon things incidental to the text, or by evasion of the real difficulties of a text.

8. *Explanation should preserve the dignity becoming to the treatment of inspired thought.* Do not explain that which needs no explanation. Avoid fanciful interpretations. Handle the Word of God reverently and honestly.

9. *Explanation should be made interesting.* Dignity and dullness should not be synonymous. Cultivate picturesque expression. Trust the common stock of biblical thought as found in evangelical commentaries and use it courageously. But do not use it in the bulk, second-hand; work it over; reconstruct it; polish it; put it through the laboratory of your own thinking.

10. *The explanation should be free from certain scholastic weaknesses.* Avoid needless use of technical terms of philology; avoid needless allusions to the authority of manuscripts and variant textual readings; abstain from a pedantic citation of commentaries, but do not pretend an independence of commentaries.

11. *An explanation should be such as to suggest naturally the proposition of the sermon.* We are often aware in listening to sermons that the gulf between the text and the proposition is not bridged in any natural and effective way. The text is explained, the subject is introduced; but neither is linked to the other. With the text in mind we listen to the proposition with surprise: with the proposition in mind

we recall the text with surprise. A good explanation will show that either the proposition is contained in the text, or that the proposition is naturally suggested by the text.

12. *In a topical sermon the explanation should, if possible, be such as to bring the text to bear directly upon the conclusion.* It is often of great value to be able to use a text in the application of a sermon. To repeat it, to urge it home as containing the germ of all that has been said, even to show that text and sermon are in the same line of thought, and the application of one is therefore supported by the other—this is often of great force in the conclusion. Sometimes this adjustment of explanation to conclusion is not possible, because not natural. The application of the sermon may flow more naturally from the body of the discussion than directly from the text.

13. *The explanation should be varied on different occasions.* Have no stereotyped method of exposition. Do not always philologize by verbal criticism. Do not always explain descriptively. Do not always tell of the author of the text, his character, his condition, his history. Do not always cite parallel passages, nor always paraphrase. We must have variety if we have fitness: then we gain a virtue in variety itself.

E. The Location of the Explanation

The locality of the explanation relative to other parts of a sermon will vary according to the character of the sermon. In an expository sermon explanation forms the body of the discourse; while in a textual sermon the explanation may often be divided. In the textual sermon each clause of the text is a division of the sermon and will be explained in the development of its own division. In the topical sermon, and in some textual sermons, the explanation may sometimes form an introductory division by itself. This will often be the natural method of explaining a very difficult text, or a text which is commonly misinterpreted, or a text which is severely contested. But in a topical sermon the explanation will, more frequently than otherwise, be a preliminary to the proposition. As to which shall come first, the explanation or the introduction proper, when both are needed, no rule is practicable: follow the homiletic instinct. Sometimes this will give the precedence to one, sometimes to the other, and sometimes it will intermingle them.

CHAPTER IV

THE INTRODUCTION

A. Introduction Defined

THE introduction is that part of a sermon which is intended to prepare an audience for agreement in opinion, and for sympathy in feeling, with the preacher on the subject of the discourse. In exact definition we must distinguish between preliminaries in general and the introduction proper. For example, the exposition of a text is not necessarily introtion; it may render an introduction unnecessary; but in itself it is distinct. An introduction is a specific process which resembles no other in the composition of a sermon. The problem in the introduction is how to bring the audience and the preacher's subject together. The characteristic idea of an introduction is that of preparation of the minds of the hearers for the message. This should be done naturally and gradually, not abruptly, convulsively, startlingly. We must always have an introduction, even though it may sometimes be without words. Certain equivalents for an introduction exist, which may enable a preacher to dispense with the form of it in words; but it is so because the preparatory process is otherwise accomplished.

Introductions require the highest skill. In them the rarest qualities of thought and style are practicable, the best originality, the greatest beauty of illustration and finish in diction, the utmost delicacy of execution. The effectiveness of the whole sermon often turns upon the quality of the introduction. An accomplished preacher will disclose his trained mind and practiced pen clearly in this part of the sermon. The introduction, therefore, seeks to bring the audience mentally and sympathetically up to the same level as the preacher, so that what is in his mind and heart may be floated over to the minds and hearts of his hearers.

B. The Specific Objects of the Introduction

These may vary, but usually the objects listed below are included.

1. *To secure the good-will of the audience toward the preacher.* Power over the majority of men is largely the power of person. Even physical presence is an important factor in the creation of influence with the popular mind. Men of large frame and erect carriage have the advantage over diminutive men in competitive labors. But mental and moral qualities are more powerful than physical presence in securing the good-will of an audience. They truly constitute the man. This power of person with an audience is a legitimate object of homiletic culture. We should never take the attitude that we can speak the truth effectively no matter what men think of us. A pastor's chief cultivation of the power of person must be outside of the pulpit, in his home, in the homes of his people, in his study, in his closet, and in his business relationships.

2. *To stimulate the attention of the hearers.* Generally this is the chief object of the introduction: often it is the only object. Pastors labor under disadvantages in seeking the attention of an audience. They have to speak so frequently,

their audience does not change much, the popular familiarity with the subjects of preaching, and the indifference arising from the depravity of hearers, all are disadvantages to be overcome.

Therefore, an introduction should avail itself of the natural curiosity which hearers feel in the beginning of a discourse, because it is the beginning. The fact that it is the beginning pricks the ears. The first sentence of a sermon and the last are always interesting. It is wisdom, therefore, to assume the existence of the interest of curiosity and to use it. Begin with an audience where they are. Do not go behind or below them in search of them.

The introduction should direct interest to the subject in hand. Assuming that an interest exists, give it an object. Guide the interest of the hearers in the right groove, to the right end. Therefore a series of disconnected remarks can not form an introduction. Such a series may be interesting; it may be original; it may sparkle with scintillations of genius; but, for want of coherence and aim, it is not an introduction. It leads nowhere: it ushers in nothing. An introduction is a tributary for the subject, and for that only it exists. And, an introduction, which, though aimed at the subject in hand, does not reach it squarely, is a defective introduction. It does not hit the target in the eye, but falls short, or to one side, or goes beyond it.

Furthermore, an introduction should lead the interest of hearers to the subject in a natural way. The announcement of the proposition should never raise a question in the minds of the hearers as to the way the preacher came to it.

3. *The third object of an introduction is to dispose the hearers to receive favorably the message of the sermon.* Men are often interested when not convinced, nor even predis-

posed to conviction. Much depends on securing the favor of an audience to the person of the speaker. If a man wins us, he will the more probably sway us. Much depends on suppressing, by the introduction, the consciousness of difference of opinion between preacher and hearer. Let us avoid militancy and belligerence in introductions. If we set up imaginary opponents and beat them down, probably nobody in the audience will be hit, but we create temporary opposition. Men will bristle in self-defense if we approach them bristling. Such an error in preaching is as profound an error rhetorically as it is morally. We should always try to begin on common ground with our hearers, even if truth should compel us to leave it. We can often find common ground by citing authorities whom the hearers trust, or by quoting a popular proverb. Much depends also upon a temperate expression of truth in the introduction. Extremes of opinion are not winning anywhere, least of all in an introduction.

C. The Most Important Characteristics of a Good Introduction

1. *Simplicity.* This is the first in order and the first in importance. Simplicity is obviously sacrificed by abstruse trains of thought, by prolonged argumentation, by an obviously elaborate style, or utterance of impassioned feeling. You must kindle the fire before you can use it. We should reserve the sensibilities of an audience till a place is reached where an appeal to them will be timely. If the audience should be in an excited state of feelings due to current happenings, then we may begin where the audience is.

2. *Unity.* Unity of introduction includes all that is essential to oneness of impression. A true introduction is always an aim and a shot. No part of a discourse should be more

intensely one in its impression. There may be diversity of material in the introduction, but it must all be unified around the subject. All these objects of your introduction point inward to that. All materials must be subordinated to one main idea as indicated by the subject or proposition. There must be no wavering between alternate subjects. Fix the subject to start with, define it, and stop all wavering of preliminary thought.

3. *Directness of approach.* Several things are needful to secure this quality of directness of approach to the subject in hand. Do not begin at a needless distance from the subject. Strike into the trail of a subject at the outset, just at the right point of ease in drawing hearers after you. Make progress in thought with as great rapidity as the nature of the subject will permit. Make everything clear as you proceed, but press on. Rapidity of introduction is desirable for the sake of brevity. Eliminate all non-essentials. Rapidity of approach also stimulates interest. It is a stimulus to the preacher and to the hearer. Rapidity of approach indicates mastery of the subject, and enlists the confidence of the hearers. Directness of approach is not abruptness. It will not do to come to a subject by a leap. This is not a homiletic advantage but only an indication of a mental vacuity. There must be a gradual approach to the subject yet no tediousness, repetitiousness, or slothfulness.

4. *Congruity with the character of the sermon.* The introduction should be characteristic of the subject in hand. Do not burden the introduction with general religious ideas not explanatory of the meaning of the text, not needed by the coming subject, yet good in themselves. Keep the introduction true to its own character as a tributary. It should not be superior to the rest of the sermon in rhetorical qualities.

The stimulus of the introduction, whatever be the source of it, should be proportionate to that of the discussion, and therefore much inferior to it. A sermon should never be remembered by the splendor of its exordium.

Congruity of introduction may be sacrificed by anticipating in it material which belongs to the main body of the sermon. The proper locality of materials in a sermon is a matter requiring very delicate adjustment. Vital forces may depend on the question of location. We should not prove the proposition in the introduction, but only arrive at its statement. Proving the proposition is the work of the body of the sermon. The introduction should resemble the body of the sermon sufficiently to suggest it. The porch should match the house, the vestibule should suggest the temple. Let logic usher logic, beauty herald beauty, grandeur prefigure grandeur, solemnity foreshadow solemnity.

Congruity of introduction implies that it shall cover everything in the sermon which needs introductory remark. Every thing in the discourse which needs any preparatory work should, if possible, be prepared for at the beginning. The complete introduction will also prevent the cumbersome mixing of preliminaries in the body of a sermon. Some times we notice a multitude of remarks scattered here and there, which are strictly introductory in their character. We should seek to say in the introduction as nearly as possible everything of a preliminary nature which must be said anywhere. We thus clear the deck for action.

5. *Modesty.* Modesty should extend to all parts of a sermon, but it is especially necessary in the introduction. Modesty requires a sensible reserve in allusions to the person or character of the speaker. Three needless obtrusions are the preacher's professional authority, his own religious experi-

ences, and an excessive use of the pronoun "I." Modesty will indicate proper respect for the audience. This can be shown by carefulness of dress, freedom from excessive care to make things plain, absence of arrogant insinuations, elimination of flattery, and a kindly treatment of the prejudices of the hearers. True modesty also requires freedom from certain affectations of excellence in the preacher, freedom from an affectation of humility, and particularly freedom from excess of modesty. Modesty is a robust virtue, never apologetic, cringing, or self-depreciative.

6. *Suggestiveness.* The introduction should lay a moderate but positive tax upon the intellect of the hearers. Set them to thinking early in the progress of the sermon. Thus you most effectually prepare them for a vigorous train of thought in the sequel. The narrative form of introduction is suggestive, as is also the descriptive form. A good narrative or description is a truth visualized. Raciness of introduction may be gained by originality of thought. Original thinking is self - diffusive. One such thought becomes everybody's thought, and instantly sets the reproductive energy of nature at work. You can never waste a new thought upon an audience if you succeed in making it clear. Suggestiveness in an exordium can be promoted by tact in utilizing the circumstances of an occasion. While suggestiveness is a virtue, over-suggestiveness may be a vice in an introduction. We need to guard against an over-crowded introduction, too much raciness, or too much hortatory material.

D. Varieties of Approach

For the man who preaches in the same place many years, the most serious defect of introductions will likely be a want of variety. Certain hackneyed introductory thoughts and

phrases are apt to creep in habitually. What are some methods of achieving variety?

1. *The first is to approach a subject without an introduction.* An explanation of a text, and the derivation of a theme from it, may sometimes be the whole of the preliminary material. There is no introduction proper. This might be called the expository approach. When used, it should be chosen for its specific congruity, never for its convenience only. This substitute for an introduction should not often be used, and certainly it should never be used when we can not defend it as the best approach possible.

2. *The introduction applicatory of the text; not explanatory but applicatory.* To this class belong all forms of introduction designed to modernize the practical bearings of the text. Whatever you say in making that transfer of the text from application to the Jews or the Apostles to people of today, and in aiming it well, is an introduction applicatory of the text. This practice is often necessary.

3. *The introduction intensive of the text by comparison with other Scriptures.* You may wish to show that your text is not a solitary one, but that it is supported by many other passages. This is not truly explanation, nor confirmation, but rather intensification.

4. *The introduction explanatory of principles involved in the discussion.* You propose to show the necessity of the atonement from the convictions of the human conscience. You introduce the subject by remarks upon conscience as a source of evidence of truth. You affirm that it is a reliable source; that it is one form of divine relevation; that the common sense of man recognizes its authority. You proceed to interrogate it, and to learn what its teachings are as to the forgiveness of sin.

5. *The introduction narrating facts necessary to an appreciation of the subject.* The narrative looks forward to the subject, not backward to the text. A story of a rich man failing to find permanent satisfaction in his riches might lead up to the subject of full satisfaction in Christ.

6. *The introduction illustrative of either facts or principles involved in the discussion.* Start out with a present-day illustration of the biblical truth you propose to discuss.

7. *The introduction commendatory of the subject.* This may be done either by a direct assertion of the importance of the theme, or by comparing it with inferior topics, or by showing that eminent authorities have considered it important, or by leading up to it by cumulative steps.

8. *The introduction connective with the preceding discourse.* This applies particularly to serial preaching.

9. *The introduction which is a condensed review of another subject related to that of the sermon in hand.* This might be a newspaper or magazine article.

10. *The introduction which requests the attention of an audience.* When the Lord's table is set before an audience, the introduction to your message is there objectively before them, and you may need no other preliminary than to ask them to follow in a meditation on the Lord's Supper.

Work on your introductions. Seek a wide variety. Make them rich, inviting, quickening.

E. Composing the Introduction

The introduction has been called a preacher's cross. It is the most easy subject to criticize, but the most difficult to execute. As an aid in composing the introduction, we wish to give a few suggestions.

1. *Define to your own mind the specific object of the introduction.* Try to determine exactly what your particular theme needs in the way of introduction. The effect is as painful to the hearer as to the preacher, if you labor to introduce a subject which needs no introduction. It is equally painful to see a preacher laboring at the wrong object in an introduction, or laboring in an introduction without an object.

2. *Review the growth of your subject in its working upon your own mind.* Such a review will commonly suggest the best material for an introduction of the subject to an audience. That which has clarified a subject to you will help you to invent ways of clarifying it to others. As you review your struggles with the subject, you will be more sympathetic with your audience. You will not be likely to ask them to leap a chasm under which you were obliged to dig a tunnel.

3. *Compose the introduction with the whole discourse in view.* The subject, the discussion, the application, all the structural elements of the sermon, should be before you. The living spirit of the sermon, too, must be in you. A lifeless introduction is often lifeless for the reason that it has no living union with the subject in the mind of the preacher. It is only a piece of dead timber nailed to a living tree.

4. Therefore, *do not compose the introduction till the plan of the whole discourse is outlined.* Write out a plan of the entire sermon from text to finis; adjust the form of the proposition; devise the outline of the argument; invent the chief illustrations; shape the application; decide upon the method of closing: in a word, get everything before you which is to be introduced. It is perhaps better not to write the body of the sermon in full before composing the exordium,

for by that time the preacher has lost the introductory mood. This is a matter for experiment.

5. *Throw yourself into the work with enthusiasm.* Prepare an introduction as if every thing depended on the first impression. Maintain a keen appreciation of the signficance of first impressions. Not only strike when the iron is hot, but make it hot by striking.

Chapter V

THE PROPOSITION

A. Proposition Defined

THE proposition is that part of a discourse by which its subject is defined. It tells the audience what you intend to say about your topic. It marks out the course of your sermon along one particular line as it stems out from the subject or topic. The proposition states the thing to be proved or the question to be answered in the sermon. It includes but is not restricted to what is termed proposition in the nomenclature of logic. It embraces all varieties of rhetorical form by which a subject is indicated to the audience. The proposition is usually an affirmation, or a declarative sentence, but it may be interrogative.

The proposition is to the discourse what the heart is to the physical system. The relation is organic. It is the sermon in a nutshell. A proposition, and a proposition studied, and a proposition stated, and often a proposition finished in elaborate and compact form, is a most vital part of pulpit discourse. Though but a fragment in form, it is an index to the whole style of thinking which underlies the form. Without it, the most valuable style of thinking is impracticable in the pulpit; and with it, all styles may be at command.

B. The Necessity of a Proposition

Whether or not a sermon has a proposition formally stated is a question of more than form. It is a question of the inner quality of preaching. Leave out the proposition, and you have shallow and effervescent preaching. Use the proposition, and you have thoughtful, solid, elemental preaching. There are several reasons why every sermon should have a declared proposition.

1. *The oratorical instinct of a good speaker demands that he shall have a proposition.* Expressed or latent, the proposition must exist, else a preacher cannot speak to the point.

2. *The instinct of good hearing demands, on the same principle, that a speaker shall state his proposition.* How can the hearer know which direction the speaker intends to go unless he defines his subject in a propositional statement?

3. *The nature of a spoken address is such that it needs a statement of the theme.* In hearing, do we not instinctively, and soon after the commencement of an address, ask ourselves, What would the speaker be at? What is the aim? Where is the target? If it seems to be concealed, are we not restless till it is discovered? This mental experience of a hearer is only the silent demand made upon the preacher that he shall have a proposition, and that he shall announce it.

4. *The popular mind is peculiarly dependent on knowledge of the theme as an aid to unity of impression.* Performers on the tight-rope steady their whole muscular system by fixing the eye intently on a point in the distance. The knowledge of the subject at the outset will be to the power of attention what the fixed eye is to the muscles of the gymnast.

5. *Pulpit subjects are by their very nature liable to confusion in the popular conceptions of them.* The inquiry before us ceases to be a question of forms: it deepens into a ques-

tion of things. The common mind is burdened with the sense of sameness in the discourses of the pulpit. Preachers seem to repeat themselves. Hearers judge sermons by their own consciousness of the effect of sermons. Sameness of effect is often, in their judgment, equivalent to sameness of materials. If the shot fall fast and long in one spot, they lose the sense of succession in the sense of continuity. The tendency, therefore, is to a fusion of the popular conceptions of truth. Such fusion is confusion. Thoughts on religious themes run together, and themes themselves are blended in the popular theology.

The pulpit, therefore, must divide and define and identify religious thought in the popular experience. Men need to be taught by the pulpit to know what they believe, and why they feel, what emotions are legitimate to one truth, and what to another, and why they differ. Truths needs to be individualized by analytic preaching. To achieve this education of a people, preaching must use freely the expedients by which a logical mind naturally makes itself understood in the expression of strong thought on great themes. We must generalize less, and analyze more; exhort less, and argue more. We must divide and isolate, and specify and concentrate our most profound conceptions of elemental truths.

Therefore preach very little in the general, and much in the detail. Preach little on truth, and much on truths. Preach rarely on religion, but constantly on the facts, the doctrines, the duties, the precepts, the privileges of religion. Divide, discriminate, define, sharpen, clarify, doctrine by doctrine, duty by duty, fact by fact, till the whole map of Christian faith is outlined and clear. You thus gain the power of pointed preaching.

6. *The use of that class of expedients to which definite propositions belong,* and of that kind of preaching to which they are a necessity, tends to form and consolidate the theological faith of a people. The question, then, of the formal statement of the themes and the salient thoughts of sermons is not a question of taste only. Still less is it a question of forms only. It affects vitally a policy of thought; and its decision is an index of a policy in preaching upon which success depends. You must have centers of discussion which shall be visible. To make these centers visible, you must make them luminous; to make them luminous, you must have definite statements of them which shall penetrate the understanding, and remain in the memory. In no other way can you get possession of available forces with which to work upon the popular life.

All this comes by intuition to a live man who understands his mission in the pulpit. Yet even such a man may hang a mill-stone around his own neck by cultivating an antipathy to the natural forms of logic in the construction of discourses for the pulpit. By banishing those forms from his sermons, he may banish the things they express; and then strong, positive, argumentative preaching is no longer possible. This is one of the things of which you must have the forms, or, in the long run, you can not have the things.

7. *Yet the best analytic methods of sermonizing will sometimes fail to define truth in the popular theology.* The perils of the pulpit in this respect are nearly all on one side. A hundred sermons fall still-born from the pulpit because of their pointless structure, where one repels hearers by excess of angularity. You will very soon begin to observe, in taking note of the effects of sermons upon your audiences, that a structure which seems needlessly formal to you often is not so to them. Hearers so easily fail to follow the preacher's trend of thought, or else misinterpret what he is saying, that clarity of thought and strength of analysis are essential.

The popular mind is both intelligent and ignorant. The same individual mind may be both. The masses of men have sagacity without culture. Whatever intuition can teach them they see with the eye of an eagle. But whatever depends on mental training, they need to be taught line upon line, precept upon precept. They will appreciate keen distinctions, if you once make those distinctions palpable. Gain attention to them and assent is swift. But the multitude do not originate distinctions nicely. They need statements made for them, and so made as to command their understanding.

8. *Speakers in other walks of life speak for a purpose, and hearers hear for a purpose.* From both the senate and the bar we learn the necessity of propositions. Look over the ranks of eminent legal minds, and you will observe that, almost without exception, those who command the position they hold, and hold the position they choose, are men of this type of intellectual force. Their productions when analyzed exhibit a polished compactness in the expression of vital truths which give to mere statement literally the force of a syllogism. Their propositions are proofs. They prepossess conviction.

C. May the Proposition Ever Be Omitted?

1. *Some apparent exceptions are not real exceptions.* The occasion itself, or the text of Scripture under consideration, or the public announcement of a sermon theme beforehand. each or all of these, may render the formal announcement of a proposition unnecessary. But these are not real exceptions

to the principle. The proposition in each case is there, but not formally announced.

2. *Shall a proposition be omitted for the sake of politic concealment of the aim of a sermon?* No, unless it be on very rare occasions. We may well conceal an intention of appealing to the feelings of our hearers but should not conceal the aim of appealing to their intellects. Intellect courts visible approach: sensibility evades such approach. Intellect is bold, and craves bold treatment. Sensibility is coy, and hides itself: it would be secretly won. This is human nature.

The omission of all forms of proposition is not necessary, even when the application is concealed till the end. A proposition may involve your conclusion without stating it. Your proposition may announce a theme in the general: your conclusion may disclose a specific truth on that theme. Your proposition may be an interrogative: your conclusion may be its answer. Your proposition may ask attention to some thoughts suggested by the text: your conclusion may educe results which the hearers would not have tolerated at the outset. In each of these methods concealment is wisely practiced, yet a definite proposition is stated and held as a center of interest. To withhold all form of proposition is an impediment to the policy of concealment. To withhold a proposition implies an obvious concealment, and our minds instinctively brace themselves against a hidden purpose on the part of the speaker. Therefore, the perfection of art requires that the policy of concealment be itself concealed, and this demands some form of proposition be announced as a center of interest to the mind of the hearer.

D. What Principles Should Regulate the Substance of a Proposition?

The substance of a proposition may be regarded in three relations—the relations of its elements to each other, the relation of the whole to the text, and the relation of the whole to the sermon.

1. *The elements of a proposition should be so related to each other that they shall be susceptible of unity of discussion.* A good discourse is a structure—one structure, a whole, not a congeries of alien particles.

Nothing is a sermon which is not a structure. Every part of the sermon must fit into the structure. Every part should gravitate to every other part. The demand of this grows out of the very nature of persuasive speech, and is inevitable in every mind.

The foundation of unity of discourse must be laid in unity of proposition. The parts can not gravitate towards each other without resultant forces which meet in a center. There must be centripetal action. The first constructive idea we can form of a discourse must be an idea of its proposition.

If a discourse has no unity of theme, a good hearer instinctively struggles to create it and insert it as the discourse proceeds. The elements of a proposition must be so related to each other as to promote obvious unity in the sermon. A sermon may be devoid of unity even though the proposition is not; but it surely will be devoid of unity if the proposition is.

Unity of proposition does not restrict freedom of discourse, but rather admits of every variety of discourse which has an object. It restrains only discourse at random. From the nature of the case, there must be four fundamental varieties of unity in discourse, and therefore in propositions; and there can be no more. First, a proposition may admit of a logical unity of discourse, where the aim is to prove something. Second, a proposition may be adjusted to a didactic unity of discourse, where the aim is explanation, not proof. Third, a proposition may be fitted to a picturesque unity of discourse, where the method is illustrative, and the unity is precisely the unity of a good painting. Fourthly, a proposition may be adjusted to a purely oratorical unity of discourse, where the object is direct persuasion. Argument, explanation, illustration are found in the sermon, but only as subordinate elements. These four radical varieties of unity, the logical, the didactic, the picturesque, and the oratorical, are exhaustive of the analysis of unity in discourse. These are the fundamental varieties and there can be no more. The test of the unity of a discourse is this: Can its materials be all brought under the cover of a proposition, which, in any of these senses of the term, is one?

Such unity as this does restrain heterogeneous discourse, but the Holy Spirit is the author of order, not of confusion. He no more prompts to disorderly, inconsecutive discourse, than he prompts to raving. If a preacher's materials can not be built into one kind of a structure, for one purpose, they ought not to be thrust together at one delivery.

2. *The subject of the proposition should be congruous with the text.* It is an excellence peculiar to the themes of the pulpit that they can be formed in keeping with inspired authorities. Proposition and text should sustain each other. If the proposition is the trunk from which the body of the sermon expands itself, the text is the root from which, in some sense, the proposition should grow.

3. *The substance of the proposition should be identical with the body of the sermon.*

(1) A proposition should not comprise more material than can be impressively discussed in one sermon. This caution is necessary because of the tendency of imperfectly disciplined minds to indulge in excessive latitude of subject. What is the result of such excessive propositions? Usually the discussion falls short of the proposition. Sometimes, however, the sermon is sacrificed to the preacher's strain to equal his proposition. It ceases to be a discourse: it becomes an abstract of a discourse. Elaborate it may be, but as a table of contents is elaborate. Arguments are stated which there is no time to amplify. Facts are affirmed which there is no room to prove; or proved, which there is no space to illustrate. The structure is not a discourse, but only a mammoth skeleton of discourse.

In other cases, the result of excessive latitude of theme is the sacrifice of the vitality of the sermon by commonplace details. Generalities in thought naturally take on hackneyed forms in style. These flow in monotonous succession like the fall of a millstream. Restriction of subject assists the invention of original materials. Youth often believes that vastness of subject will insure abundance of materials. Just the reverse of this is true in fact. If your inventive power is sluggish, restriction of theme will stimulate it: if it is active, restriction of theme will give it scope. Invention exercised on a restricted proposition is microscopic. It discovers much, which, in ranging over a broader surface, it would lose. It is penetrative. It goes in to the heart of a theme. The mind labors perpendicularly, not horizontally. The result of such labor is that kind of discussion which impresses the hearer with the conviction that the marrow of the subject has been reached. The preacher speaks from a full experience of its richness in his own mind. Such preaching seems inspired.

Observe a few illustrations of this stimulus to invention from restriction of theme. Do not certain packed propositions quicken your thinking upon them in the very hearing? "Religion is the best reason of State;" "Good intentions are no excuse for bad actions;" "Concealment of sin is no security to the sinner." Do not such aphoristic propositions invite thought? "Faithfulness in present duty qualifies for higher functions;" "The instruments which God chooses are not such as man would have chosen;" and, "The temptations attending opportunities of doing good." Who does not feel that he could enjoy constructing a sermon on any one of these themes? The singleness of them is interesting, and the compactness of them is quickening. A broad, general proposition has the effect of being flabby and sprawling with room to spare.

Moreover, restriction of subject has a tendency to freshen stale truths. "Go thy way for this time: when I have a convenient season, I will call for thee:"—a stale text is this, often used. Thousands of discourses have been preached from this text on procrastination of repentance. How shall we elude a stale sermon from this text? Think about this text carefully in its context, and from it educe this proposition, "Men who are deeply interested in religion as a theory often revolt from it as an experience." Are not the stale text and the commonplace subject, by such restriction of range, freshened to the thought of both preacher and hearer? This vitalizing of stale themes is one of the great arts of the pulpit. We cannot avoid such themes, and we dare not treat them in the rut of centuries of preaching. We must vitalize the theme, and the best way is to retrench the theme for the sake of concentration of force.

Restriction of subject is of special value to the interest of doctrinal preaching. Doctrinal preaching and dull preaching are not synonymous. Doctrinal preaching must be sharpened, made alive, and infused with those elements essential to vivacity. One such element is the rhetorical expedient of restricting the substance of the theme for the sake of stimulating the invention of the preacher. We should never attempt too much in one sermon. Rarely should a standard doctrine of theology be presented entire in one sermon. Usually such sermons are heavy and crowded with material. They are abstracts of theological treatises and lack the oratorical elements. If you will preach upon doctrines as you preach upon duties, by analyzing the themes in bulk, and retrenching the range of single topics, and thus securing opportunity to use your materials as you would use other means of moral impression, you will find no other themes of the pulpit so popular as the doctrines of the Christian faith. Doctrinal sermons come alive when you give yourself room to put life into them.

However, occasions may demand the more comprehensive treatment. It may seem necessary to present in a single bird's-eye view the whole plan of a doctrine, or even a group of kindred doctrines, in one sermon. All such occasions are exceptional. They are justified, if at all, by some speciality of aim. They are not thorough discussions of all the truth presented. They would have no moral force if they were the common product of the pulpit. They need to be preceded and followed by more analytic discussions requiring restriction of theme.

(2) The substance of a proposition should not comprise less material than is sufficient for impressive discussion in one sermon. We should not select diminutive or puny themes.

A preacher's mind is in a molecular mood in selecting such themes. They are scarcely crumbs from the Master's table. That can not be a comely structure in which immense or profound thought hangs as a pendant to a proposition of which the first and last impression is trivial. The dignity of the Christian pulpit must be sustained by worthy subjects of discussion. No other spot on earth is environed by associations of such dignity as a Christian pulpit. Its subjects should bear proportions to such associations. The first impression of the proposition of a sermon, and the last, should be such as to sustain the respect and reverence of men. For this end a certain bulk of substance is essential. If a theme is too restricted, it may more properly be a division of a sermon than a proposition. Again, time in the pulpit is invaluable. No preacher can afford to squander an hour of it. The vital, the necessary, the imperial topics of homiletic discussion are more in number than the opportunities of preaching in any one lifetime. Multitudes of such themes throng every pulpit. Great themes are always waiting for a hearing, and every preacher should keep a notebook or file of fertile texts and suggestive themes. Select then the choice themes of discussion, and only those. Of important themes, choose the most important. Of prolific themes, give place to the most prolific. Deal only with superlatives. Apply mercilessly the law of natural selection. Let only that live which must live. No pulpit has room for diminutive propositions. The great themes may seem hackneyed, yet the range of suggestion of such themes is immeasurable, and the opportunity for versatile treatment is immense. The great subjects, though few, never lose their power if treated by a fresh mind. The need of them never grows old. Put your soul into them and they are always fresh.

(3) The proposition should not contain other material than that which is discussed in the sermon. A common defect is that propositions do not express the real topics of discourse. The proposition may promise one thing, and the sermon may realize another. Do not propose to discuss the privilege of fellowship with Christ, if the sermon deals with the duty of fellowship with Christ. Do not propose to consider the nature of repentance, when the discussion bears on the duty of repentance. Keep always in mind that a proposition is a promise: it demands foresight of your means of payment. Again, the unity of the proposition and the unity of the discussion should coincide. It lies in the nature of persuasive discourse to have a point of unity. Such discourse is a structure; it must have aim; that aim must gather into itself all the forces of impression which the discourse creates. There can be no perfect discourse without the coincidence of the unity of proposition and unity of discussion. A proposition is but a figurehead to a sermon, if it does not suggest the true center of interest in the sermon.

In judiciary decisions it is a standing principle never to anticipate a case, never to expand a principle beyond the necessities of the case in hand. Such should be the policy of the pulpit in the construction of propositions. Specify: specify: so far as the aim of the discourse admits, always specify. Propose no other than the thing to be realized. Volunteer nothing in the proposition which the sermon will not redeem. Meet in the proposition the exact demand of the discussion; no more, no less, no other.

E. The Forms of Propositions

The form of a proposition is a striking feature in the face of a sermon just as is the nose in the human countenance. Both express character.

1. *Certain fundamental distinctions of form in the statement of propositions.* There is the distinction between logical and rhetorical propositions. A logical proposition affirms or denies. A rhetorical proposition states a subject for affirmation or denial. Any subject can be stated in either form, but it may make considerable difference which form is used. Logical propositions are distinguished as affirmative or negative in form, and any truth may be stated either affirmatively or negatively, yet we may see very positive rhetorical reasons for preferring one form to the other. Rhetorical propositions are distinguishable as declarative or interrogative in form. The declarative form of proposition is most commonly used, but there may be good reason to throw the proposition into the form of a question to which the divisions constitute the answer. Again, all these forms of proposition may be further distinguished as simple, complex, or plural forms of proposition. A simple proposition mentions a subject only, with no appendage af relations. A complex proposition pursues a subject into its relations and yet retains singleness of form. A plural proposition specifies a group of topics which have unity of subject, but not unity of form. Generally, it is better to hold to the simple or complex proposition and avoid the plural form.

In a good proposition every word is vital to the structure. The locality of every word is of moment to the whole. The relations of each word to every other, the arrangement of words into clauses, the number of words, and the syntax of the whole are essential subjects of criticism in the construction. A proposition is the embodiment of emphasis: it is all emphatic. Great care should be given to the formulation of the proposition.

2. *Certain principles which should regulate the forms of propositions.*

(1) The form of a proposition should be characterized by as great a degree of simplicity as is consistent with a full statement. The prime virtue in a perfect statement of anything is its simplicity. Let the proposition be a statement, a full statement, and nothing but a statement of the thing in hand. We should avoid the use of words of unintelligible or doubtful meaning to the hearers, such as scientific terms, abstruse philosophical expressions, and technical terms of theology. If a preacher employs in the construction of his propositions and divisions only those technicalities of theology which the Bible has originated, and omits those which are the pure product of the schools, he will be on reasonably safe ground. Preachers must remember that themes which seem elementary to them may be obscure to hearers. Abstractions, to a mind which feeds upon them, become like concrete realities. But, for the purpose of discourse to an audience, there is great power and great beauty in calling things by their simple names.

Simplicity of propositions may be promoted by avoiding figurative forms of statement. A proposition is not an explanation, it is not an appeal, it is not an illustration, and it is not primarily an argument: it is a statement and nothing more. The defect in a figurative proposition is that it is not the simplest form of statement. A figure may give clearness to an explanation, force to an argument, vividness to an illustration, eloquence to an appeal, but not simplicity to a statement. It may therefore be more pertinent anywhere else in a sermon than in the statement of a proposition or division. Literalness is essential to simplicity in any thing which professes to be a statement and nothing more.

A good proposition may be a good title; but a good title may not be a simple proposition. A title may be only a hint of the contents of a discourse; therefore it may be imaginative.

If any thing is a business in the pulpit, and ought to take on the form of plain, business-like speech, it is that calm unpoetic part of a sermon in which a preacher has merely to tell an audience what he proposes to talk about. There, if nowhere else, we should come at the intelligence of hearers by the shortest, plainest, most natural, and hence most literal way. Instead of seeking to throw around a proposition some of the draperies of venerable homiletic usage, we should rather think of the mathematical definition of a straight line.

The simplicity of propositions and divisions requires that they should not be stated in the language of popular proverbs, such as, "Honesty is the best policy." Because they are familiar proverbs they have an atmosphere about them which is not kindred to that of simple speech. They are the pert remarks of the highway. Their original dignity is gone, and now they are pedestrian and dusty.

Again, simplicity of propositions and divisions demands still more imperatively the exclusion of fantastic forms of statement. One man preaching on the text, "They know not what they do," used the proposition, "When men know not what to do, they should be careful not to do they know not what." Earnest minds have neither time nor taste for the creation of such sports of ingenuity.

Finally, simplicity in propositions and divisions requires the avoidance of extreme paradox in their forms of statement. A slight paradox is not inconsistent with a calm statement, but an extreme paradox implies excited statement.

Whitefield has a discourse on the proposition, "Persecution is the lot of every Christian." Either this is not true, or the vast majority of Christian church members are hypocrites. The truth may be expressed more simply and temperately by the proposition, "A Christian is not apt to be a favorite with the world." Some may vindicate paradoxical propositions on the ground that they paraphrase Scriptural texts, such as, "All that will live godly in Christ Jesus shall suffer persecution." We answer that texts are not inspired models of propositions. Texts are limited by other texts, interpreted by contexts, illuminated by occasions and events, qualified by the characters concerned in their delivery. Isolate them, as propositions are isolated, from these interpretative surroundings, and often they are not true. A proposition must reduce to literal and independent statement the truth conveyed by the text considered in all its intricate relations.

(2) A proposition should be as brief as it may be consistently with clearness. Propositions should not be expanded by needless synonyms. Needless synonyms may excite false expectations of the range of a discussion. Every word in a proposition is emphatic, and practically every word will attract attention. Therefore, find a use for every word included in the proposition. Neither should a proposition be expanded by needless epithets, or by intensification of the subject for rhetorical impression, or by circuitous or indolent grammatical constructions, or by repetition in varied language.

Again and again it deserves to be repeated that a proposition is a statement, and only that. To vary it, and repeat it, and reiterate it, and intensify it, and magnify it, and dignify it, for the sake of rhetorical effect, are all foreign to its purpose. A perfect proposition never needs such handling.

To inflict it on a good proposition is only hammering at the nail when it is already driven to the head.

This view leads to the further remark, that it is not good policy to lift a proposition, in point of impressiveness of structure, to a level with the conclusion. A proposition must always contain the conclusion; must, often in substance, be the conclusion; but it should invariably fall below the conclusion in impressiveness of statement. No single principle of homiletic policy is more variously applicable than this, "Leave room for increase of impression." Begin low, and work up. Leave space for rise of interest. Begin with a clear but calm statement of the truth; then set that truth to revolving; prove that truth; illustrate that truth; vary the position of that truth; disclose in light and shadow the proportions of that truth; till, as the discussion advances the hearer feels that truth, and only that. Then in the conclusion, you may assume that he feels it, and may proceed to apply it in the assurance that no language which it prompts you to employ will be an exaggeration, or will seem to be such to the hearer's quickened conscience and deepened sensibilities. But to anticipate all this in the structure of the proposition is sheer reversal of nature. It can not succeed in its aim, and it would be an injury to the discourse if it should succeed.

The proposition is often rendered needlessly diffuse by making it consist of the divisions of the sermon. That which has been termed the plural proposition is not relatively desirable. Unity may exist in such a proposition: necessity may rarely require it. But, when no necessity for it exists, its prolixity should exclude it. Do not disclose the plot of the discourse at the outset. It leaves nothing to stimulate expectation by suspense of curiosity. This is often a sufficient objection to a prolix proposition,—that it discloses too much. Instead of furnishing only a center of interest, it marks out all the radii of the circle. To justify this the necessities of the subject should be imperative. When the gist of the subject can be made palpable without it, the plural form is an encumbrance. Only the gist of the subject is needed in a proposition.

(3) A proposition should be as specific as it can be consistently with brevity. Specific statement limits the range of a discussion; it concentrates attention; it stimulates interest. To this end, the logical form of propositions should generally be preferred to the rhetorical form. As an example, the rhetorical form might be, "The divine government," while the logical statement would be, "The divine government is founded upon mingled justice and benevolence." A proposition should also convey a complete idea in itself. Again, the specific quality requires that the proposition should not generally be stated in the exact language of the text. The text might as well stand alone, as to reproduce its ideas in a proposition that adds nothing in modern and vivacious style.

The specific quality in a proposition demands, further, that it should not specify any thing which is not discussed in the sermon. The proposition sometimes overreaches the sermon, not by needless or irrelevant synonyms, but through inadvertence.

(4) The proposition should be framed with as great a degree of elegance as is consistent with clear and forcible expression. Finish of form often reduplicates force. The style of a proposition should comprise that rare blending and proportion of qualities which never make one think of style. To this perfection of form, elegance is essential. Elegance

requires the restriction of the vocabulary of propositions to classic English words. The usage of the pulpit has from time immemorial been unscholarly in retaining obsolete words, cant words, technical words, words never heard outside the pulpit, which deform a proposition even more than any other fragment of a discourse, because its pre-eminence of position enforces attention to them. Again, elegance of proposition demands purity and ease of English construction. That is not a perfect proposition which attracts attention by its clumsiness.

(5) The preface to a proposition should be distinct, simple, and on different occasions, varied. I refer here to the few prefatory words by which the announcement of a proposition is foretold. These are often of more importance than they seem to be. The preface should be distinct, indicating clearly that the subject is about to be defined. And it should be simple, with no parade made of it. Five things suggest the most natural variations for the preface. They are the preacher, the text, the sermon, the occasion, and the audience. Reference to any of these can be made with proper modesty and simplicity, leading up to the statement of the proposition.

See Appendix II for examples of outlines with propositions.

CHAPTER VI

THE DIVISIONS

THE divisions are the principal sections of an orderly discussion. Good discourse in the pulpit demands that a preacher shall have divisions in his own mind, and that he shall so state them that hearers shall be distinctly sensible of them.

A. The Necessity for Divisions

1. *Divisions thus formed and stated promote perspicuity of discussion.* They aid a preacher in gaining perspicuity; clear mental action works instinctively by plan and each assists the other. Divisions assist the hearer to clearness in understanding a discussion. So far from divisions being a deformity, originating in the pedantry of the pulpit, they are one of the necessities to which the pulpit has been driven by the lofty nature of its subjects.

2. *Divisions promote comprehensiveness of discussion.* They assist a preacher in collecting and arranging the material for such a discussion. Divisions also assist a hearer in perceiving and appreciating the comprehensiveness of discussion.

3. *Divisions promote unity of discussion.* They assist a preacher in preserving unity. The very effort to classify materials tends to unify them in the result. It is an excellence in divisions, that they thus stand guard over extemporaneous thinking, and shut out all that is not tributary to the result.

Still more do well-constructed divisions assist hearers in perceiving the unity of a sermon.

4. *Divisions promote progress in a discussion.* They assist a preacher in making progress. Organization achieves in discourse that which it achieves in everything else—rapidity of execution. The same expedient assists a hearer, also, in perceiving progress of discussion. Few things are so essential to impressive discourse as the sense of progress. Hearers crave the consciousness of achievement.

5. *Divisions also promote conciseness of discussion.* A perfect sermonizer will trust largely to divisions for crowding the greatest bulk of thought into the shortest time. Divisions assist both the preacher in achieving conciseness, and the hearer in appreciating a compact discussion. To make an undisciplined hearer sensible of the fact of crowded thought in a sermon, you must in some way tell him of it. Divisions do this indirectly. They call attention to one thing at a time: therefore they concentrate attention. And, they disclose all waste of words, if there be such. It is an excellence in divisions that they restrain excessive hortation.

6. *Divisions promote elegance of discussion.* Clearness of statement, finish of form, orderly succession, unity of aim, completeness as a whole, and growth in construction are all elements of graceful discourse.

7. *Divisions may be made to assist a preacher in meeting without loss of power the popular demand for brevity.* Audiences will not tolerate unduly long sermons. Preachers can not control the public taste. We have only to accept it, and to make the best of it. The task of the preacher is to compress into the smallest possible amount of time in the delivery the greatest possible amount of solid yet interesting matter. To achieve this, well-framed divisions are indispensable.

Short, crisp statements of the salient thoughts of a discourse will often save the necessity of prolix argument. Statement which carries in itself the force of argument is the style of divisions now needed in the pulpit. With such divisions to emphasize the imperial points of a discourse, you can pack into it vastly more material than can by any ingenuity be put into the same length of slipshod harangue.

8. *Divisions promote interest in a discussion.* This they do by promoting clearness, unity, elegance, and speed. The enthusiasm of the preacher is most vigorously sustained by a clear, unified, elegant, progressive plan of thought before him as a model. The act of framing such a plan creates a courageous interest in executing the details. The interest of the hearer is even more dependent upon good divisions. The sense of progress which they quicken stimulates attention; and the mental rests which they furnish relieve the weariness of prolonged attention. Even that class of hearers who are beguiled by false tastes and affectations can always be reined up to healthy thinking by a compact, racy statement of an elemental truth, like those which divisions should express. Plain sense pithily uttered will catch and hold a wandering mind.

9. *Divisions promote permanence of impression.* That is the best sermon which furnishes the most effective means of holding it in the memory. The most effective of such means commonly are the text, the proposition, and the divisions. These are the parts of a sermon which usually have the longest life. A preacher, above all others, aims at lasting impressions. He needs, therefore, as many expedients as are natural to make truth penetrate the memory.

We should cultivate that which Pascal calls the geometrical spirit. It is that bent of mind which defines, which proves, which demonstrates, which therefore affirms positively in the end. Only thus can you fairly deliver the inmost spirit of Christianity. Christianity claims to be definite, revealed, positive, authoritative. It is reason addressed to reason, and faith commanding faith. To speak to men in the full spirit of it we must geometrize. We must construct. We must be architects and builders. Sermons must be elaborated and finished structures. No other part of them should be so deftly elaborated as the inner framework. That should be a finished mechanism, even if nothing else is finished. Strength in preaching depends on no other rhetorical excellence so much as good divisions and propositions; that is, on good planning of thought. Cultivate the faculty of strong, compact, finished planning. A skeleton may not be a thing of beauty, but it is the thing which makes a body erect and strong and swift.

B. The Extent of Divisions

This should be regulated primarily by the nature of the subject.

1. *Some subjects repel numerous divisions.* When elaborate division and subdivision is applied to a simple subject, there is a sense of incongruity. A sermon of consolation to the afflicted could scarcely be minutely divided.

2. *Some subjects demand minute division.* The necessity of analysis is evident on the face of them. Subjects on which the truth is easily misunderstood or may be plausibly perverted may require numerous divisions; or truths which are open to many intricate objections often need to be treated with numerous divisions. And subjects which are very prolific of practical applications may need numerous divisions. A general rule is, that, the more severely the subject taxes

the mind, the more imperative is the need of thorough division of materials.

The extent of division should be regulated by three considerations: the character of the discussion proposed, the character of the audience addressed, and the amount of time at command in preaching. The trend in our times is toward fewer divisions rather than more. Preachers like Jonathan Edwards and Charles G. Finney used a multitude of divisions and subdivisions, many more than would be tolerated today.

C. Abuses of Divisions

Some of these are obvious.

1. *The employment of any arbitrary number of divisions is an abuse.* There is no reason to strive always for three main divisions, or four or five.

2. *A lawless multiplication of divisions is an abuse.* Never whittle a subject for the amusement of it.

3. *Generally it is an abuse to extend divisions beyond the second degree.* Subdivisions of subdivisions will rarely, if ever, be distinguished as such by hearers. We can safely have main divisions and subdivisions of main divisions, but division beyond that point is futile.

4. *Visible division is an abuse, so far as it is framed for the convenience of the speaker alone.* A good speaker must have more elaborate divisions in his own mind than a good hearer needs. Orderly discourse can not exist ideally without many invisible sections. To the speaker it is a convenience to state these visibly; but to the hearer this statement may complicate and encumber the subject.

5. *Visible division is an abuse so far as it exceeds the necessities of elaboration.* This is most frequently illustrated

in needless subdivisions. Beyond the necessities of elaboration, form becomes not only an encumbrance, but an affectation; for it pretends to an intricacy which does not exist. It thrusts upon the hearer a help which he does not need.

6. *Visible division is an abuse, so far as it outweighs rhetorical force.* In all oral speech, and especially in preaching, results depend much more on rhetorical impression than on scientific form. Science must therefore often yield to rhetoric in the structure and expansion of a sermon. The table of contents of a book may be very perfect as a scientific structure; but it is dull reading, because it has no rhetorical force. It has no expansion: it is all form. It has as little eloquence as a triangle. So a sermon may be divided and subdivided till it is little else than a skeleton. A sermon of superior materials may break down under this excess of machinery. As a scientific lecture it may be a model; but as a sermon it is arid and brittle: it wants spring, speed, wings.

D. The Materials of Divisions

Of what thoughts should they be composed?

1. *A division of a discourse should be necessary to the development of its proposition.* The proposition is the plan in germ: the plan is the proposition unfolded. Every division in the plan, therefore, should be essential to the expansion of the proposition. It should grow out of the proposition, and live upon the proposition, as a branch grows out of and lives upon the root of a tree. It should be impossible to see how the proposition in hand could dispense with the divisions in hand. To be necessary to a proposition, a division must be comprised in that proposition. Divisions should not be grafted on propositions. A divison is often relevant to a

general subject when it is not so to the proposition. It belongs to the same genus, but does not come under the species.

Furthermore, to be necessary to a proposition, a division must be founded on a real distinction from every other division. Distinction without real difference is often the defect of two consecutive divisions. Difference of phraseology is accepted as difference of thought. Difference in the materials of development may conceal the fact that there is no difference of divisions. This real distinction from every other division should be an important distinction. One variety of error is that in which a division unimportant in itself is advanced for the sake of interesting materials which can be introduced under it.

2. *The divisions as a whole should fully develop the proposition.* Not only should no needless divisions be introduced, but no necessary divisions should be omitted. Collectively the divisions should be a complete discussion of the proposition. Note that exhaustion of a proposition is not exhaution of a subject. The prolix discourses of some of the English and Scotch divines grew out of a failure to recognize this distinction. Hence their interminable divisions.

That divisions may fully develop a proposition, the proposition and divisions should be so invented as to fit together. To do this, it may be necessary to put some qualifying word in the proposition, such as, "Let us consider *some* of the reasons;" or, "a *few* of the reasons;" or, "the more *important* reasons," etc. Then your proposition is not a promise to discuss every possible reason.

Divisions do not fully develop a proposition if they do not sustain its intrinsic dignity. This is true when a profound proposition is superficially treated, when an affluent theme is meagerly treated, or when a novel subject is tritely treated.

On the standard themes of the pulpit a certain fund of popular thought exists below which a sermon on one of those themes ought not to fall. A meager sermon upon one of them should never be preached by any one.

3. *Divisions should consist of the most powerful thoughts which a mastery of the subject discovers.* Two things in this principle are to be emphasized—mastery of subjects, and the use only of selected materials. Defect in either is loss of power.

A weakness in many sermons is premature discussion. The outline reveals that the preacher is not ready to discuss that theme; he has not mastered it; he has worked in the dark. The divisions are inadequate because he has not had the subject well in hand. A more frequent evil is poverty of materials. This, too, the plan of a sermon will often discover. The divisions are not the rich products of a full mind. They are not select materials. They hint at no unspoken reserves. Sermons should embody the best materials germane to their subjects; and this, realized in any pulpit, will create a strong pulpit. In no other way can we eradicate from the popular mind effeminate and ephemeral tastes. To create strength, you must give strength. Give to your preaching the vividness of lightning, and your people will not crave the phosphorescence of fire-flies.

4. *Divisions should all be classified, if possible, upon the same principle of division.* The principle of division may be by treating a truth objectively or subjectively; negatively or positively; logically or chronologically, etc. Sometimes a mingling of different principles of division in one discourse is a necessity, but the needless mingling of diverse principles of divisions is an evil. Divisions can appear to be distinct in

form when they are not so in reality. They covertly overlap, and the preacher repeats himself, because he has not followed a single principle of division all the way through. Put all divisions in the same category or classification.

5. *Divisions should be susceptible of unity of development.* Each division should be in itself a unit, and susceptible of complete development. Therefore a division should not comprise materials which are not one in their natural impression. It is unphilosophical to consider the nature and the cause of a thing under one division. The meaning of the doctrine of the perseverance of the saints and the fact of the perseverance of the saints are two main lines of thought and should not be discussed under one division. Each requires a separate division. It is not fitting to apply a truth to Christians and to the impenitent in the same division, unless the same application is beng made to both. Certain processes can not naturally be intermingled. They may succeed each other; but they can not be blended. In constructing a sermon, attend to one thing at a time.

Yet the unity of a division may admit of obvious distinction of materials, which, though distinct, lie in one line of thought. Thus a division may propose to illustrate and prove a truth, for illustration and proof are very closely allied in rhetorical character. They assist each other. A division may treat of the depth and the breadth of a principle. These are distinct qualities, yet in unison. Depth and breadth are both measures of magnitude. The impression, therefore, is one. Unity of division may even allow the combination of certain opposites of material. Opposites are not always contradictories, as facts are not always truths. Some opposites in thought are complements to each other. Beneath the surface a hidden current unites and intermingles them. Unity of division, therefore, admits of very great diversity of materials. It demands no iron rigidity of exclusion; but is ductile, rather, to the utmost extent of natural combinations of thought. Especially is the dual division often the natural unit. The point to be watched in adjusting the materials of divisions is not the fact but the degree of diversity. Any degree is natural which leaves room for natural oneness of impression.

6. *Divisions of the body of the sermon should not anticipate those of the conclusion.* Certain materials in every discourse naturally belong to the conclusion. In an argumentative sermon, for instance, the development of the proposition, and the applications of it, are totally distinct processes. The one belongs to the body of the sermon, and the other to the conclusion. You have no logical right to apply a truth before it is proved. The divisions of the body of the discourse must in such cases keep to the necessities of logic. In an illustrative sermon, the location of materials may make a vast difference. Some materials are more intense than others. Those of the body of the sermon should be so selected and adjusted as to leave the most intense for the conclusion.

Preaching is exposed to the peculiar peril of premature applications of truth. No other themes of public discussion are so prolific of practical application as are those of the pulpit. The conclusion may be weakened by too much application in the body of the sermon. By petty distribution of impression all impression is lost. The conclusion can only repeat what it might have been, if the preacher had practiced reserve and concentration.

7. *The materials of the conclusion should not return upon the foregoing parts of a sermon, except by way of intentional recapitulation.* It is distracting and confusing for the divisions of a conclusion to return to previous parts of the sermon by the suggestion of new materials which belong to those previous localities. Finish each section of the sermon as you go. Do not come back and add postscripts later on. Sheer repetition of material may bring about this same defect.

8. *Divisions should be as suggestive as possible of the main thoughts of the proposition.* No single quality of good divisions is more valuable than this. The idea of it is that the materials of each division should be so related to the proposition as to be a reminder of it. The two should be connected by something like the indefinable resemblance often observed between parent and child. A core word or phrase or idea can usually be fitted into the proposition and all the main divisions, thus binding them easily together; but this should be natural and logical, not artificial and forced. This incessant reproduction of the proposition in the divisions can not be achieved by forms alone. The thoughts of the division must produce the effect. Things, not forms, must create it. Here, as elsewhere, that style only is good which springs into being at the command of thought. But, when the very substance of a division demands the form which embodies this suggestion of the proposition, no audience is so uncritical as not to feel the excellence. It lies in the instinct of good hearing to catch such sympathy between subject and division, and to feel the tribute of it to powerful discourse. If it is not possible to carry the central thought of the proposition over into a division, then either the proposition or the division is to be suspected of some radical defect.

E. The Form of Statement of Divisions

1. *The same principles requisite to the construction of the forms of propositions apply as well to the forms of divisions.* The practical objects aimed at are that the forms of statement be intelligible without being hackneyed, that they be interesting without being fanciful, and that they be easily remembered.

2. *The forms of divisions should be adjusted as forcibly as possible to the design of the proposition.* Visible resemblance to a proposition in the form of a division is always desirable. If it is not possible, then do not force the resemblance.

3. *Divisions should be constructed, if possible, so as to suggest each other.* When they resemble the proposition, they will resemble and suggest each other, but they will need to be arranged in some logical, chronological, or rhetorical order. Fanciful expedients, such as alliteration, rhyming, and forced antitheses, are out of keeping with persuasive discourse, and should not be used to bring about resemblances in the forms of divisions.

4. *Divisions should be so constructed as to be truthful in the connection in which they stand.* Care should be taken that nothing precede or nothing be omitted, which would render the statement as it stands practically untrue.

5. *Divisions should be so stated as to foster expectation in the hearer.* Various as the several orders of divisions are, the object aimed at in them is always the same. It is progress in intensity of moral impression. The order which best promotes this is in any given case the superlative order. Follow that order, and you can not go wrong. End with that for which the hearer's need of the discourse is most imperative.

Expectation may be fostered by avoiding needless commonplace in the forms of divisions; by concealment of the conclusion in the forms of division; by the negative method of discussion; by the interrogative forms of division; and by certain indefiniteness of form in the statement of divisions. Seek fresh expression in the statement of divisions, and avoid hackneyed statements. By all natural arts keep the conclusion secret. One of the evils of announcing a synopsis of the sermon at the beginning is that it foretells too much. It hints at conclusions, often reveals them outright. Often when we show that a truth is not this and not that or the other, it excites curiosity to know what the truth is. Similarly, a series of questions proposed and answered may keep up interest. If a speaker can hint at something in his own mind, the full expression of which he is holding in reserve, he may be able to sustain expectation.

6. *In different discourses divisions should be constructed with diversity of form.* The best forms become hackneyed by constant use. We must not follow the same general plan of constructing our sermons so consistently that our hearers will always be able to anticipate how we are going to handle a subject.

F. The Order of Divisions

The natural order of thought must be variable. Much must be left to the homiletic instinct in the selection. All we can do is to point out the chief varieties of order by which divisions may be arranged.

1. *Divisions may be arranged by an order of logical necessity.* Some materials must from their very nature precede others. Some thoughts have no logical force until others have prepared the way for them. Some divisions must necessarily rest upon other divisions.

2. *Divisions may be aranged in an order founded upon the relation between cause and effect.* No rule can be given as to which should come first in the discussion. In some cases it may be best to advance from effect to cause. Divine providence reasons with men mainly by that order.

3. *Divisions may be arranged in an order founded on the relation between genus and species, i.e., between a class of things and its sub-classes.* Here also not invariably must the genus be first considered. The order of discovery is generally from species to genus. So may be that of popular discourse.

4. *Divisions may be arranged in the order of intrinsic dignity, usually identical with the order founded on weight of argument.* The order of argument should be climactic— the weakest argument first and the strongest last. Intuitively, we should begin with the less and end with the greater in gradually ascending scale. Positive argument naturally follows negative argument; probable argument follows presumptive argument; conclusive argument follows proximate argument.

5. *Divisions may be arranged in an order suggested by psychological analysis.* A large group of the materials of the pulpit group themselves around the faculties given by the analysis of the mind. We need not use the term psychological but they are such. Intellect, feeling, and will lie at the basis of the division. We begin with the intellectual appeal, go on to the feelings, and then to the will. But again, we can not always preach in the psychological groove. The opposite order may be necessary to the purpose of the sermon.

6. *Divisions may be arranged in an order of time.* Events in historical order, biography in chronological order, hypo-

theses in the order of probable occurrence are illustrations of this.

7. *Divisions may be arranged in an order dependent on progress in the personal interest of hearers.* One of the chief aims of preaching is to individualize hearers, and to bring truth home to each man's personality in that order of progress which most stimulates individual interest. This might be from the remote to the near, or from truth of infinite range to the truth of present consciousness.

If varieties of order should conflict, then we should follow one order straight through and not combine two orders so as to create confusion.

G. The Mode of Announcing Divisions

This concerns chiefly two things, the use of numerical announcements, and the use of other prefatory words. By either method the chief objects of the announcements are three—intelligibility, congruity with the feelings of the hearer, and permanence in the memory of the hearer. With these objects in view we readily see the propriety of certain principles which are flexible in their application.

1. *Divisions should be so announced that transition shall be distinctly perceptible.* Numerical forms need not always be used, but we may also use such transitional words as "again," "further," "moreover," "once more," and "finally." The object is to call attention to the fact of transition. Whatever does that announces a division sufficiently. Some discussions require numerical forms. Transitions must often be emphasized in order to be observed. Colloquial usage employs the numerical forms freely.

2. *Divisions should be so announced as to preserve congruity with the nature of the materials.* There should be congruity between emotional materials and the severest of logical forms. Numerals are adapted to explanatory and argumentative divisions. For hortatory, and often for illustrative materials, the less formal preface is sufficient, and therefore the more becoming.

3. *Divisions should be so announced as not to be confounded with each other.* General divisions and subdivisions may easily be confounded, if both are introduced numerically. A good general rule, therefore, is to number your general divisions only, and announce your sub-divisions by the less formal method.

4. *Divisions should not be needlessly announced by a preliminary synopsis at the beginning of the discussion.* We have already noticed this as often a needless form of the proposition. But frequently it is a more needless appendage to the proposition. The subject is formally announced, and then the entire outline of the discussion is proclaimed. In very rare cases this may be a necessity.

5. *Divisions should be so announced as not to disclose prematurely the character of the conclusion.* A conclusion may be foretold, not only by the substance of the divisions, not only by their form, but also by their prefatory announcements. Whatever else must be foretold, the character of the application should never be revealed till the moment of its instant use.

6. *Divisions should be so announced as not to deceive an audience respecting the destined length of the discourse.* Never express or hint at false promises of brevity. A preacher

is under obligations of honor to his audience in this thing. He is master of the field. His hearers are helpless under the imposition of his flux of words through which they peer in vain for the end. They can not rise and rebuke him for his prolixity. The most popular quality of preaching is brevity. If a sermon does not possess it, do not exasperate an audience by promising it.

See Appendix II for examples of outlines with propositions, divisions, key-words, and core-ideas.

CHAPTER VII

THE DEVELOPMENT

A. Definition of Development

THE development is the unfolding of the salient thoughts expressed in the divisions, and no more. The work of development is the composition of the sermon as distinct from the planning of it. It is the doing of the thing proposed in the plan. It is the clothing of the skeleton of the sermon with the elements of effective discourse. It is in this sense that I employ the word in discussing the development as one of the constituent parts of a sermon. When you have chosen a text, evolved a proposition, and outlined a plan of a sermon, the bulk of your work is, in the majority of cases, yet to be executed. You are now to amplify, to expand, to unfold, to evolve, to fill up, to enlarge upon, to develop-- whatever you may call it; and the thing is clearly distinct from any other process concerned in the building of a sermon. To many preachers it is a work of much greater difficulty than is involved in any other process. It sets invention at work more severely, and calls into service a greater variety of mental powers, than does any other part of a discourse.

B. The Foundation of Good Development

The foundation of a good development is laid in certain things which precede its execution.

1. *The possession of the right quantity and quality of materials.* If your mind is filled with only anatomical materials, you must fail in the attempt to make them live in a

breathing sermon. A certain degree of fullness of mind with right material is essential to forcible development. Sparse thoughts invite feeble utterance, even of that which a man has to say. Thoughts must crowd thoughts in order for any thing to come out with force. It is the full fountain which bubbles to the surface.

When a division of a discourse presents a blank to your mind which you will not know how to fill, set your mind to thinking upon it. Fix the mind on the thing in hand; check rambling thought; have done with reverie. This is the first and vital thing. Then group together all that you do know of the matter. Use that something that you do know as a bait to suggestion. Follow it into its natural surroundings. Write it down, and thus obtain the suggestive aids of the eye. A pen in hand, or the typewriter in operation, and an eye on a written thought are marvelous allies to the thinking power. Use in this matter whatever of the common stock of thought on any subject you find in present possession. The stock will grow upon your hands inevitably. The law of your experience will be that to him that hath shall be given.

If the above procedure fails, resort to suggestive reading for a while. Read any thing which stimulates thinking. You have probably discovered in your library one or two authors whom you never can read for a half-hour listlessly. They are awakening powers to your powers. Your mind always springs at their bidding. Turn to such volumes, and use them for the stimulus which they furnish. The thing needed is a mental awakening and uplifting which shall bring within your range of vision a broader intellectual scenery. Thus uplifted, the mind obtains inspiration, and, thus inspired, it may go back to the thing in hand tremulous with inventive ardor.

We should never forget the ultimate source of wisdom. It is never amiss, and often is the only remedy, to fall on the knees in earnest prayer for heavenly inspiration and help. After casting one's self contritely and utterly on God, there will often come a noticeable lift and surge of inventive thought.

2. *A decision as to what kind of treatment the thought in hand requires.* We need to decide whether or not anything in this division needs to be explained, proved, illustrated, or applied by direct hortation. If more than one of these is needed, then we must decide how many, and in what proportion. Consciously or unconsciously every mind in the act of successful composition does propose to itself and does answer these inquiries. How shall a preacher judge when to explain, when to prove, when to illustrate, when to exhort, and when and how to intermingle these processes? We must judge, in part, by the genius of the subject; in part, by the character of the audience; in part, by the demands of the occasion; in part, by the recent proportions of your preaching in respect to its rhetorical character; in part by personal tastes, information, and moods.

3. *The third of those prequisites to a good development, which lies back of its execution. is a certain mental dexterity which comes from practice only.* In every art there is a knack which is never a gift. It is the fruit of apprenticeship. How to do the right thing never comes wholly from knowing what to do. It comes, in part, from doing. It comes from failures, awkwardness, blunders, despairs, infinitesimal beginnings of success, happy hits which are never repeated, and the slow growth of faculties which a man can never outrun in com-

posing. Your mind grows with perpetual increments of the knack of doing.

C. The Chief Characteristics of Good Development

1. *Unity*. A division amplified is a discourse in miniature. Its singleness is essential to secure speaking to the point. Unity is especially sacrificed by an unconscious discussion of different things with one heading, and another form of the same defect is a confusion arising from resemblance or sameness of words. Also, unity of development may be unconsciously sacrificed by the confusion of thought springing from the indefiniteness of figurative language, or from pressing to an extreme the suggestions of analogy.

Another class of errors which mar unity consists of intentional digressions. Everything is intentional digression in which a speaker consciously dallies with the thing in hand. This error may take the form of discourse without construction, or may consist of talking against time, or may take the form of excessive illustration. We should never illustrate for the sake of the illustration, its beauty, its novelty, its eccentricity; nor for the sake of rhetorical display; nor for the entertainment of an audience. Another intentional digression may take the form of a deliberate change of theme.

2. *Pertinency*. Several points may be noted as things which will illustrate themselves in your practice. Strict unity will commonly secure pertinency of development. If discourse holds to one thing, it will probably be the one thing which the division proposes. Rarely will an educated preacher state one thing, and then at the very start discuss another thing. The arrow when on the string is usually aimed rightly.

Guard unity by intense composing and pertinency will probably follow.

Irrelevancy of material often concerns only its location. Remarks are often relevant to a different division from that under which they occur. Not the choice of material, but its location, is in fault. It is relevant to the subject, but belongs there, not here. Also, irrelevancy of material is often limited to isolated remarks. It seldom covers whole pages consecutively. It blotches them over with single remarks in which the preacher has written with momentary languor; and the progress of thought is impeded accordingly. Such remarks are to discourse what excessive friction is to machinery. Intense discourse does not tolerate these fragmentary impertinences, and intense impression is always impaired by them.

The habit of precise and intense thinking will tend to adjust the details of a development as rigidly as it plans the outline of a sermon. Every sentence of a sermon is a subdivision of something. The same law of close thinking should govern the species as the genus. Yet just here occurs the collapse in the power of many sermons. Good plans are feebly executed. Many minds think vigorously in outlines, but languidly in details. They become enervated when they pass from the work of the scholar to the work of the orator. Sturdy thinking should hold its own to the end. One reason that the Puritan preaching of the seventeenth century was so vivacious, in spite of its prolixity, was that its thinking was so vigorous. It could suspend argument to interweave illustration, anecdote, biography, history, any thing which would illumine the train of thought, without a break in that train, and without the creation of any sense of irrelevance.

This was done with such unconscious adroitness that the sense of consecutiveness was seldom lost.

Rhetorical pertinence often requires that a development shall receive a more vigorous treatment than is demanded by the mere connections of logic. Logical sequence may be indirect and yet unbroken. Rhetorical force may be so diluted by indirectness as to evaporate in commonplaces. Logic deals with the intellect pure and simple; rhetoric deals chiefly with the sensibilities. Intellect may thread the mazes of a languid development, provided that logic be kept unbroken; the sensibilities can not always do that. They do not readily obey the threadlike and tortuous lines of connection. They require obvious continuity. They are stimulated by high coloring. They sometimes need contrasts of coloring in which the mind passes back and forth with unconscious speed. To preserve absolute pertinence of material in such a process is a far more difficult achievement than to forge the links of an argument. It requires more nervous thinking power.

3. *Completeness.* The development is to the division in hand what the divisions collectively are to the proposition. The one should exhaust the other. Completeness of developmen, then, may obviously be sacrificed by the omission of a necessary link in the argument, or by an inadequate statement of the strong point in an argument, or by a want of clearness of connection. Accuracy of connections is often slighted. Certain words, sentences, paragraphs, are simply connectives. By themselves they are forceless; yet without them discourse would be impossible. Without them, men would commune with each other in ejaculations. Carelessness as to clearness of connections causes a sense of inconsequence in the progress of thought.

Completeness of development is further sacrificed by a want of forcible presentation. Materials may be unified, pertinent, connected, and yet may fail for the want of vividness. Generally the defect is the lack of illustration. Pure argument and pure didactic explanation seldom do themselves justice before the popular mind. The illustrative element in popular discourse is necessary to completeness, because it is necessary to forcible impression. Frequently the only lack in a development is not in thought, not framework, but in its temperature. It is constructed of good material, and is well-jointed, but it wants glow. It needs to be recomposed to gain intensity.

4. *Conciseness.* Conciseness means that the preacher speaks with quick advances. He says what he has to say and is done with it. Thought, structure, style are all condensed. The crannies and crevices of discourse are packed full. The effect in utterance is a combination of weight and speed, and that combination is always power like the power of a cannon-ball. We need much of this kind of discourse in the pulpit. Yet conciseness in preaching must be subordinated to completeness of discussion. Conciseness is a relative excellence; it must be adjusted to subject and audience. Some themes will not bear extreme compactness: they need amplitude. Oral discourse in its very nature requires a certain bulk of expression. Proof may not be understood if expressed in naked syllogism, nor may explanation be grasped if given with mathematical brevity. Illustration is often needed, as much to gain time for the thinking power of a hearer to rally around a thought, as for the direct purpose of making it luminous.

Conciseness of development is promoted by cultivation of the condensing power. A condensed style is concise development. We should cultivate a taste for short words, for Saxon words, for unqualified substantives, for crisp sentences. Also, conciseness of development depends largely on a wise retrenchment of materials. Eliminate superfluous thoughts, say only necessary things, depend on selection, not on conglomeration of materials, and conciseness is inevitable. Avoid needless explanations. Assume all that can safely be assumed of the intelligence of the hearer. Avoid proof of things which can safely be assumed. A wise preacher studies when to argue, and when to dictate. Do not try to prove that men are sinners, that time is short, that death is certain, that eternity is important, that truth is right. The most stupendous truths, and sometimes the most bitterly contested, must generally be assumed in preaching. The being of God, the necessity of revelation, the authority of conscience, the truth of the Scriptures, the facts of heaven and of hell must commonly be proclaimed by assumption.

So of the countless minor threads of thought which make up the woof of sermons. Speak by authority when there is no need of argument. Assume as much as possible of existing belief in the hearer's mind. Avoid preaching to absent opponents. Similarly, avoid illustration beyond the necessities of the case. The common stock of thought in sermons contains much which needs no illustration, more which needs but momentary illustration, and but little which needs illustration piled on illustration. Finally, let us avoid useless repetitions. Some repetitions popular discourse must have. Repeat, if necessary, for emphasis. Practice variations on one thought, if necessary, to gain time for growth of interest; but, as soon as your point is gained, drop it and pass on. By thus retrenching superfluous materials, and materials of secondary worth, depending on necessary things, conciseness of development is achieved as a matter of course. The sermon then becomes massive and solid.

5. *Order.* If style is "the right words in the right places," then good development might be defined as the right thoughts in the right places. There is always a natural order of thought. Oratorical instinct goes far to determine this; but it may be assisted, and at the same time, obeyed, by attention to four very simple things.

(1) Finish one thing at a time. Say connectedly all that is to be said on a given thought. Concentrate discourse long enough to carry the point, then pass on.

(2) Aim deliberately at continuity of thought. Every thought in a good discourse is a link in a chain. Every thought looks forward and backward, and is naturally preceded by something and followed by something. Seek this natural continuity and execute it.

(3) Avoid capricious lines of association. Do not bring together odd and dissimilar materials. The undisciplined mind works in tangents, and has no orbit. The instinct of logic which is in every mind, is constantly overruled by hysteric impulses which begin with no aim and end nowhere.

(4) Aim at increase of intensity in the progress of the development. Every vigorous composition has more or less of climax in the arrangement of its materials. Sermonic materials intrinsically are such as to be susceptible of climax. They have gradation in their power of interest either to the intellect, or to the feelings, or to both. Follow this order and you always have the natural arrangement.

6. *Proportion.* The development of each division as a whole should be proportioned to that of every other division.

Proportion should be governed by weight. Give the largest bulk to the weightiest thought. That which is most essential to the aim of the discourse is weightiest: necessities take precedence of luxuries. Therefore, search out the organic elements of the discourse and see to it that they have ample room in which to expand. Give space to the heaviest arguments, the critical explanations, the most necessary and speaking illustrations, and the most intense materials of persuasion.

It is essential to begin with reserved force. Never expand a division thriftlessly. Many sermons are spoiled by the undue bulk of their first divisions. Because a division is first, and perhaps because of a lurking fear of lack of material, the preacher inflates it beyond its relative worth; and all that coming after is overcrowded. We should begin warily. Hold strength in reserve; look to the end; and measure resources and time. Then concentrate at the vital points. Never fear poverty of thought. The best things will suggest thought when you come to them in the emergency of discussion. Never amplify, therefore, merely because amplification just then and there is easy. Reserve the most robust handling for the necessary materials.

The development of each division by itself should be proportioned in all its parts. On a miniature scale, a single division is a discourse. It is a structure which has its beginning and middle and end, as an entire sermon has. An argument or a principle should not be so amplified that the application is cramped. An illustration should not be so dilated that the thing illustrated is narrowed to a point. We must discover the focal point of exigency and shape every thing so as to converge and concentrate at that point.

CHAPTER VIII

THE CONCLUSION

A. The Function of the Conclusion

THE theory of the conclusion presupposes a theme discussed, which is now to be applied to something. The intense practicalness of a sermon is hinted in the characteristic idea of its ending. That is not a sermon which is intellectual discussion pure and simple. A conclusion may explain, illustrate, prove, persuade, or all combined and intertwined. It may be the most complicated process in the whole structure of the sermon. It is susceptible of the most varied and ingenious methods of procedure. However, a conclusion is not necessarily restricted to the chronological termination. Paradoxical though it seems, the conclusion may be other than the *finis* of a sermon. Its characteristic idea is not the chronological ending, but the rhetorical end.* It is the result which the sermon is made for. Its characteristic idea of application permits its distribution throughout the body of the sermon, in place of its concentration at the close.

B. Causes of Weakness in Conclusions

1. *Lack of spiritual consecration in the preacher.* The first demand of the preacher is that he be an eminently holy man.

---

*Dr. Phelps treats conclusion and application as quite similar. Many authorities say that the conclusion is the final part of the sermon, while application is the personalized and focalized claims of the truth upon the hearers and may occur anywhere in the sermon. Conclusion and application are not identical. The first is a part while the second is a function.

Eloquence in all its forms is built on, or more significantly is built in, intense character in the man. Any type of religious experience which deadens a preacher's personal faith in the truth he preaches may create a paralysis equivalent to that of downright unbelief. Nowhere is a moral counterfeit so sure to be detected as in the pulpit. Not only is it true that God is not mocked, but the people are not mocked.

2. *An overemphasis on the intellectual as distinct from the emotional and executive effects of preaching.* Sermons may be literary models and yet be deficient in unction. Unction is thought so clothed in emotion as itself to reproduce emotion. An over-estimate of the intellectual processes in preaching does not necessarily produce the most profound intellectual sermons. On the contrary, it may and often does result in the most lifeless of dead levels as respects original thinking. When pastoral visitation and counseling is neglected, there is likely to be an overemphasis on the intellectual in preaching.

3. *A morbid fear of fanaticism* may be another cause of dilution of the applicatory force of preaching. It is not easy to decide which is the more disastrous to a preacher's power over the consciences of men—to be a fanatic, or to preach in servile fear of being one. Culture itself is a breakwater against fanatical surges, but should not become a barrier to the inflow of rational enthusiasm.

The most destructive disease of the ministry is satisfaction with other successes than those of saving souls, and building up a sanctified church. Nothing else equals this in its power to undermine an evangelical pulpit. On the contrary, nothing will so fire a preacher with enthusiasm and spiritual unction as to preach with the purpose of bringing sinners to repentance and building up saints in the faith. Such sermons naturally abound in application and appeal.

4. *Impractical theological views.* Theological theories unfriendly to rational uses of truth tend to enervate the applicatory power of preaching. A working theology in the pulpit must possess three elements—freedom from contradictions to itself, consonance with the necessary intuitions of the human mind, and harmony with the Scriptures as a whole, and as the unlettered mind reads them. Doctrines which will not bear these tests of truth, no man can use effectively in preaching. Such doctrines as the theory of a limited atonement, the theory of a sinner's inability to obey the commands of God, and the theory of the untrustworthiness of the human reason in matters of religion are examples of doctrines unfriendly to pulpit power. Much might be said in defense of these theories, and has been said by able and godly men, but these theories are not rational elements of persuasion in preaching. Persuasive power is not in these doctrines, and they can not, by any rational processes of speech, be galvanized into resources of persuasion by any rational being who can be induced to accept them intelligently.

C. The Necessity for Intensity in the Applicatory Uses of Truth

The evangelical theory of preaching always assumes in practice certain facts and principles, no matter what it may be in the abstract. Godly preachers of all schools of theology, who are intent on the saving of souls, always act on the assumption that these things are true, whether consistently or not.

1. *The extreme emergency in which the gospel finds men.* Evangelical preaching addresses men as lost beings. The

emergency is real; the peril is imminent. The most tragic of catastrophes is not only in prospect but is actually occurring all the time all around us. We come to our work with this idea uppermost in our thoughts of what we have to do.

2. *The sufficiency of the provisions of the gospel to save men.* This is as real as the necessity of salvation in the evangelical theory. The provisions are ample to meet the emergency. The world is a wreck surrounded with lifeboats. It is a lost battlefield, with reserves at hand which are ample to reverse the fortunes of the day. It is a world on fire with the windows of heaven opening over the conflagration. This too we believe. We come to our work with the conviction that the loss of a soul is never a necessary catastrophe.

3. *This work of saving souls is a practical business.* We do not concede that it contains a scintilla of romance. It is a plain, prosaic business of real life, as truly as the navigation of the sea. We come to our work with the conviction that we have a just claim to the approval of the common sense of men, in concentrating our strength upon the work of saving souls.

4. *Preaching, above all other instrumentalities, is divinely appointed to success in saving men.* The gospel proclaimed by the living voice has pre-eminently the divine sanction. Not the press, not the universities, not the libraries, but the pulpit is the chief agency concerned in the development of divine decrees to this end.

5. *The philosophy of the work of the evangelical theory of preaching is in entire accordance with the laws of the human mind.* Not only is success in preaching practicable, not only is it ordained of God, but the rationale of the

process by which it achieves success contains nothing contradictory to the laws of the human mind, or suspension of those laws. Persuasion by preaching is achieved by the very same means and methods of speech by which men are successfully moved by eloquent address on other than Christian topics of thought. The pulpit claims no exemption from dependence on natural laws. While holding firmly to the necessity of empowerment by the Holy Spirit, we do not suppose that this encourages us to neglect or abuse the arts of speech. We use those arts, depend upon them, look for success in them, as if we had no other hope of success. Such a view must inevitably work out in intense applications of truth in practice. Directness, pungency, versatile invention, studied adjustments of truth to character, ingenuity in discovery of the uses of truth, all find a necessary place in evangelical preaching.

D. Should Applications Ever Be Omitted?

Usually the application of truth should not be omitted. Some apparent exceptions to the general principle are not real exceptions. In serial preaching or evangelistic preaching, each sermon in a series should be a unit and have some application then and there, even though the cumulative power of application is withheld until the end of the series. When a preacher breaks down with emotion and cannot make his application, the most powerful of all applications is made. The silence of suppressed emotion surpasses all eloquence. Speech then may be silver, but silence is golden. If a sermon is closed with prayer instead of an appeal to the hearers, if it is genuine prayer, it is the equivalent of an application.

A real exception occurs when the discussion points to a hackneyed application as the only natural one. Then it may be well to omit all applications. Some themes are most natu-

rally treated in only one way, and hearers know what to
expect when we discuss them. In such a case it may be breath
wasted to reiterate the hackneyed application. The value of
the soul, the duty of repentance, the certainty of death, are
themes of this kind. Who could make a novel appeal on
these themes? The best thing might be to surprise the audience by making no appeal. Assume that the hearer's conscience is preaching. Surprise him by your silence since you
cannot by your preaching.

Both the real and the apparent exceptions to the general
principle before us depend for their impressiveness on the
infrequency of their occurrences. They can not be genuine
if they are frequent. Habitually employed, they take on the
appearance either of trickery or of insensibility.

E. Should Application Run Through the Whole Sermon or Be Compacted at the Close?

1. *The compact application at the close is frequently
demanded by the logical necessities of the discussion.* The
argument may not be completed until the close of the
sermon.

2. *The compact application at the close is more natural to
any elaborate discussion.* An elaborate discussion demands
continuity of attention to the thing in hand. It is unnatural
to break such a train of thought for the sake of an appeal to
the sensibilities of hearers. Severe thought and intense feeling
both tend to continuity, not to rapid interchanges. Neither
is a flexible thread of tow; neither can be woven as with a
shuttle. Mental oscillation is natural only when the mind
is at play on the surfaces of thoughts. .

3. *The compact application at the close is the more favorable to concentrated impression.* Continuous application

whatever be its advantages, must have this incidental drawback, that it divides force. Delay often reduplicates the force of the application when it comes. Further, concentrated impression is often the only possible impression. Spiritual lassitude is so common that often the only way to overcome it is to concentrate the force. Brief, sharp, condensed processes from beginning to end are among the only possible expedients of impression.

4. *The compact application at the close is the more secure against the danger of exhausting the sensibilities of hearers.* Nothing else is so flat as an appeal which moves nobody. Hearers are often injured by applications of truth which fall upon exhausted sensibilities. The compact application is less liable to exhaust and thus disgust the sensibilities of the hearers. No man has sensibility to waste. To work upon sensibility monotonously, leaving the will no chance to throw itself into executive duty, is the surest way to benumb sensibility. The wise preacher will be wise and apply truth as a soldier fires who has but a limited supply of ammunition. Efficiency of shot is more important than frequency of shot.

5. *The continuous application may, however, be sometimes required or advisable.* A hortatory discussion is nearly all applicatory. An expository discussion which is not severely critical may need continuous application. A biographical or historical discussion also falls in this category. Instances occur in which practical application grows out of the very roots of a text or a theme. The applications are immediate, obvious, urgent. Not to make them would do violence to the natural uses of the subject.

Exception to the general rule of compact application may be created by peculiarity of occasion. During times of religious excitement, or revivals of religion, delicate junctures and critical moments may occur when a direct appeal in the midst of a sermon may then be the instrument of a soul's conversion. Also, the character of the audience has some bearing on this point. An audience of children may need the continuous application, as may also an audience of undisciplined minds. They have little power of sustained attention and almost no power of abstraction. We would conclude, therefore, that the less elaborate the sermon, or the less cultivated the audience, or the more emotional the condition of the audience, the more readily is the continuous application admitted or required.

F. What Are the Fundamental Elements of a Conclusion?

1. *Recapitulation* and *appeal* are two such elements as recognized by ancient oratory. Either or both were deemed fitting to popular discourse.

2. *Inference, or remark,* is a third element added by the usages of the pulpit. The intense practicalness of the work of preaching has created the foundation for the use of inferences, or remarks, or lessons. Preaching never discusses truth for the sake of discussion; never illustrates for the sake of display. The homiletic instinct is to put it to as large a range of uses as possible.

The use of the inference, or remark, brings to practical bearings a large range of abstract themes which can not be applied in any other way. Such themes as the nature of the atonement, the deity of Christ, the personality of the Holy Spirit can be discussed with exactest logic without touching a conscience or moving a heart, yet through inference they can be applied practically. By inference from them truths of richest and sweetest flavor flow out to every conscience and every heart. The great object of preaching is to bring the gospel home to real life by showing at how many points it touches real life. The inference is a valuable device for showing the prolific nature of truth in practical application.

Inferences also deepen impression by presenting a practical truth through logical processes. A truth inferred is a truth proved. Practical logic is the strongest form of application. Then inferences often assist impression by introducing truth unexpectedly. Hearers concede the process of discussion without foreseeing the results. It is often wise to bring in those truths most displeasing to the human heart by way of inference. Inferences have a further value in that they invite the hearer's participation in the process of application. A truth inferred invites a hearer to perform the process of inference in his own mind. Anything is valuable which draws the hearer into the circle of activity in the reception of discourse.

G. On What Principles Shall We Select and Combine Recapitulation, Appeal, and Inference or Remark?

1. *On the basis of the congruity of conclusion with discussion.* Not all discussion admits of recapitulation. Likewise the nature of the discussion may invite or reject the inference and remark. Make the conclusion sympathetic with the discussion. Recapitulate, infer, remark, appeal—one or all—as may be requisite to evolve most richly the applicatory force which is latent in the body of the sermon. No matter where the discussion began, it must end with that which is natural to the process which leads to the ending.

2. *On the basis of progress of moral impression. A* hortatory sermon is frigid if ended with inference, because an

appeal is in itself more intense than inference. Recapitulation may be too cool a process to follow an impassioned argument. The closing division of an argument may be so intensely wrought that immediate appeal derived from that division only may be all that can make an increasing impression.

3. *On the basis of variety of conclusion.* The chief peril of the pulpit in applications is monotony of form. Therefore, do not always recapitulate, nor always close with inference, nor always appeal. Nature craves variety.

H. What Qualities are Requisite to a Good Recapitulation?

1. *Brevity* is first. Recapitulation requires this, for recapitulation is synopsis. It is the discourse in miniature.

2. *Restriction to foregoing materials* is essential to a perfect recapitulation. It is a purely logical process and gives no room for new material, or a new expansion of the old. It should be conducted with the utmost severity of restriction to the materials already presented.

3. *Perspicuity* is essential. The whole force of recapitulation is lost if it is obscure. The advantage of good divisions in a sermon comes to view in their recapitulation. Clear, compact, forcible divisions fall into line beautifully in an epitome of the discussion.

4. *Climactic order* should characterize the recapitulation. Generally this will be the order of good divisions; but if, for exceptional reasons, it is not, it should be the order in the closing rehearsal. Climax appears grandly in a good synopsis. The rapidity of its utterance, the conciseness of its style,

its compact reproduction of the whole discourse in miniature, may disclose the logical energy of the sermon with a concentration and vividness that the discussion did not possess.

5. *Variation of language in restating the divisions* is sometimes desirable. The elegance of a recapitulation may often be enhanced by varying the language by which the divisions were stated in the body of the discourse. Variety of style reveals mastery of thought, and is especially expressive of ease of thought. Hence it is natural that recapitulation should often vary the forms of the original statement. But such elegance of variety should never be sought at the expense of perspicuity.

6. *Thoroughly memorize the recapitulation* in extemporaneous preaching. This is self-evident. A failure of memory at this point is equivalent to a failure of logic, and is highly embarrassing to both preacher and audience.

I. What Qualities are Requisite to the Construction and Development of the Inference and Remark?

An inference is a logical sequence. A remark is a suggested sequence. A lesson is an observation which serves as a warning or encouragement. A few basic principles should regulate them.

1. *They should be legitimate sequences from the body of the sermon.* The excitement of sermonizing may deceive a preacher as to the logical and natural relations of his theme. Applications may seem obvious to him because of his immersion in his subject which are not apparent to his audience. The appropriateness of inferences, remarks, or lessons, should always be obvious. The authority of the pulpit with hearers

depends largely on the reputation which preachers establish for the integrity of their logical power. Logical reasoning power takes priority over other intellectual qualities in giving the pulpit the respect and confidence of the people.

2. *They should be forcibly deduced from the discussion preceding them.* Legitimacy of deduction is not the equivalent of force. A perfectly logical inference may be far-fetched, and a perfectly natural remark may be feeble. We want the practical results of a discussion in striking lights. The conclusion must be selective in that it seizes upon the strong points of the discussion and only those. Practical applications should never be a conglomeration, but a careful selection of characteristic and forcible truths. Some applications are trite because derivable from a large variety of sources. We must avoid sameness of applicatory remarks. There is an art then in constructing applications so as not to represent sameness but diversity of truth. Effective preaching is very largely the art of putting things. It is not invention nor discovery so much as the apt placing of familiar things.

3. *They should be developed without needless formality of statement.* A certain formality may be necessary in the body of the sermon in handling divisions and transitions, but this should be relaxed in the application. The applicatory process must be flexible, its transition easy, its forms as ductile as may be consistent with perspicuity. Some of the old English preachers had an excessive multitude of applicatory inferences and remarks quite stiffly and formally indicated.

4. *Develop them by the use of interesting materials.* Barrenness of treatment is nowhere else so great an evil as in an application. Interest elsewhere is of little use if not sustained here. We cannot trust in the elaborateness of a dis-

cussion alone for the impression of a sermon. The preacher should especially seek raciness of closing thoughts and the magnetism of last words. All is lost if, after a preacher has explained lucidly, proved forcibly, and illustrated vividly, he then is dull, trite, commonplace and uninteresting in his applications.

5. *Avoid fantastic materials* in remarks, inferences, and lessons. That is an ill-formed or ill-trained mind which revels in eccentric applications. Odd laws of suggestion are weak in practical results. Above all other intellectual qualities in practical affairs, men prize good sense. They crave to be sensibly appealed to. They demand to be treated like men of sense and by men of sense.

J. How Should Appeals Be Conducted?

1. *They should be founded on the strongest material which the sermon contains.* An appeal is intrinsically the most intense form of speech to a hearer, and should never be built on petty items, or things incidental to the main channel of discussion. The strongest material should be brought to the front in the conclusion, so that it can be naturally used as the basis of the appeal. The appeal is the soul of the sermon, and the organic life of it ought to pulsate there. Therefore the most powerful of resources should be put to use there.

2. *Appeals should be aimed at feelings as distinct from conviction.* It is one thing that a hearer should believe that he ought to feel, but it is a different thing that he does feel. Therefore to produce the conviction is not necessarily to produce the feeling. To move the feelings, the exclamatory and excited style is usually not necessary. Appeals based on plain truth, solid facts, sound principles, clear arguments,

can be very effective. When these factors are properly manipulated they make their own appeal. Silent emanations from them go forth through the whole discussion, softening the feelings and winning the affections, and preparing them to respond with reduplicated volume to a few unimpassioned words of exhortation at the close.

3. *Appeals should be aimed ultimately at the executive faculty of the soul.* Appeal should not rest with conscience alone nor with emotions alone. To arouse emotions and stop there is as unphilosophical as to address truth to the intellect alone and pause with that.

4. *Appeals should always be pointed toward vital acts of religious duty.* They should press upon hearers the things most essential to salvation; they should persuade men to the discharge of the most critical obligations. Sometimes the unsaved are exhorted to pray, to read the Bible, to ask the prayers of others, to attend meetings, and other things which are secondary acts. In the Scriptures impenitent men are never exhorted to do anything preliminary to repentance. One and but one thing is to be done—to repent; nothing else takes the place of it; nothing else assists it; nothing else includes it; nothing else approaches it. Human nature unregenerate is prone to acts of religious substitution under the goading of an aroused conscience. Therefore, under such impulses, the commands of God are easily displaced and obscured in the impenitent mind. It behooves us to guard men against deceptive substitutions. I do not say that they should never be allowed; in themselves they may be innocent; but the wise policy is to make little use of them. Exalt above them that which has a decisive meaning. Keep in the foreground the one definite act by which the soul chooses God.

Treat everything else as relatively of no moment. If men will not repent under such appeals, then press home again the fundamental ideas of the Gospel which are the natural inducements to repentance. Set the whole firmament ablaze with the glow and heat of these eternal verities.

5. *Appeals should be specific in their basis and their aim.* The point from which they spring should be well defined, and the point at which they strike should be equally so. Appeals should be reined up to specific duties by clearcut convictions and intelligent emotions. In the Scriptures, it is not the sinfulness of sin, nor the beauty of holiness which are topics of appeal; but more frequently it is the guilt of covetousness, of pride, of lying, of unbelief, of evil-speaking, of licentious imagination; and the dutes of almsgiving, of honest weights, of self-sacrifice, of prayer, of repentance, of faith. The strong points and the sharp points of Christian truth are the very points which inspired preachers use most eagerly.

6. *Appeals should not be unnaturally passionate nor weakly pathetic.* Nothing cools the feelings of an audience more effectually than to see a preacher beside himself while they are comparatively tranquil. While appeals should not be violent, they should be earnest. The degree of earnestness with which the appeal should be pressed depends on the intellectual culture of the hearers, the strength of the material in the sermon, the mood of the audience at the close of the discussion, and the guidance of the Holy Spirit.

7. *Appeals should be so constructed as to imply the expectation of success.* Hopeful men are successful men in this realm. An expectant appeal implies a good opinion of the hearer, implies a preacher's confidence in his own cause, implies personal fellow-feeling of the preacher with the

hearer, and implies the preacher's assurance of the presence of the Holy Spirit.

8. *Appeals demand a natural delivery.* Nowhere else is the theatrical, the hysterical, the violent, the awkward, so out of place as in the appeal.

9. *Appeals should be prepared and spoken under the sway of genuine feeling* on the part of the preacher. Most of the defects in appeals arise from fictitious emotion. Genuine emotion is, to a large extent, a law unto itself. Artistic counterfeit appeals are usually frigid, and betray themselves by artificiality or rudeness. Let it be noted also that an appeal, which is genuine in the composing, should not be preached, if it is not genuine in the delivery.

10. *Appeals should not be developed at great length.* Sensibility from its very nature does not bear long-winded appeal. Appeals can be interspersed with didactic remarks and illustrative incidents to relieve an audience of unremitting exhortation.

11. *Appeals should possess unbounded versatility.* Appeals should be varied as to the class of sensibilities to which appeal is made, as to the truths upon which founded, and as to rhetorical structure.

12. *Appeals should be uttered without forewarning.* All forewarning of appeals puts hearers at once on the defensive. They gird up themselves and feel secure from the attack. The element of surprise is of great practical value in any part of the sermon, but especially so in appeals.

Chapter IX

STYLE *

S TYLE is the general term by which we designate the qualities of thought as expressed in language. The pith of
this formula is that it builds style upon thought, not upon
expression alone; yet not upon thought alone, but upon
expression as well. Two popular misconceptions of style are
that it is sophistry, or expression used to mislead; and that
it is ornament, or expression used for display. Both of these
assume that style is all on the outside. Essentially style is
from the inside, for style is thought. Qualities of style are
qualities of thought. Forms of style are thought in form. Not
only is thought primary, and expression secondary, but
thought is absolute and imperial. Expression is a dependent
entity. This principle is basic. A writer of superior mental
force, starting with this principle alone, might in time work
his way by the sheer force of original thinking to supreme

---

*This chapter is a condensation of the book, *English Style in
Public Discourse*, by Austin Phelps, Charles Scribner's Sons,
New York, 1883. This book has 351 pages and was considered an
outstanding contribution to the subject. Prof. Henry Allyn Frink,
Ph.D., of Amherst College, refers to Dr. Phelps' book as "one of
the most valuable works that we have on the subject which it
treats," and condensed it to 204 pages in his 317-page book, *Rhet-
oric, Its Theory and Practice*, published by Charles Scribner's
Son's, New York, 1895. This chapter has also been checked with
Prof. Frink's condensation.

perfection in literary expression. Yet, starting without it, a lifetime of criticism and experiment could not create a style of tolerable quality.

The four things basic to the fundamental qualities of style are thought, language, the speaker, and the hearer. Out of the relations of these four things the fundamental qualities of good style grow. I find seven qualities to be fundamental in the study of style. Out of the relations of thought to language grow (1) *purity* and (2) *precision;* out of the relation of thought and language to the writer or speaker grows (3) *individuality;* out of the relations of thought and language, and the speaker to the hearer, grow (4) *perspicuity,* (5) *energy,* and (6) *elegance;* and out of a fit selection and due proportioning of the qualities already named grows (7) *naturalness* of style. All other qualities naturally fall into the rank of tributaries to these. We shall consider all these qualities except *individuality,* and that is hardly a proper subject for study, since the more one strives to gain it the less he will have of it. Individuality is a quality of style which comes unbidden. It can not be produced by force of will, nor acquired by studious discipline.

A. PURITY

1. *Purity of English style may be specifically defined by several memoranda,* of which the *first* is, that it relates to three things; viz., the form of words, the construction of words in continuous discourse, and the meaning of words and phrases. The *second,* therefore, is that it requires three things; viz., that the words should belong to the English language, that the construction be accordant with English idiom, and that words and phrases be employed in the senses recognized by good English authority. The *third* is

that, therefore, the violations of English purity are offenses against the three departments of scientific grammar.

2. *The standard of English purity of style is determined by two principles*: (1) that the laws of language are the proximate standard of purity; (2) that usage must be the ultimate standard of purity.

3. *Usage is restricted by the influence of the laws of a language.* These laws or principles are: (1) our ultimate standard of purity should be the present usage; (2) that which we accept as authority should be the national usage; (3) the usage to which we appeal for our authority should be reputable usage.

4. *The most important violations of a pure style are known as the barbarism,* the solecism, and the impropriety. A barbarism is a violation of purity in the form of words; a solecism is a violation of purity in the construction of words; an impropriety is a violation of purity in the meanings of words and phrases. We now proceed to note some of the violations of purity of usage.

(1) Purity is violated by the use of the obsolete in language.

(2) It is violated by the coinage of novelties.

(3) It is violated by the needless importation of foreign contributions to the language. We commit a barbarism if we import a foreign word when an English word will express our thought as well.

(4) Purity of style is further impaired by the needless use of provincialisms. National usage is our standard, and that is not pure English which has only sectional authority.

(5) The most unscholarly violations of purity consist of vulgarisms. Slang falls into the class of vulgarisms. Anything falling below the standard of reputable usage would be a vulgarism.

5. *The preacher should seek to do more than merely to make himself understood.* He may be understood even though he uses coarse and impure language. There are good and sufficient reasons for seeking purity of style as the best vehicle of being understood.

(1) Literary authority is uniformly in support of purity as the foundation of the most effective style.

(2) A pure style is tributary to the most perfect perspicuity of expression. The surest way to be understood is to speak your pure mother-tongue.

(3) Purity is tributary also to the most forcible style.

(4) Pure English has an intrinsic superiority for the purposes of religious discourse. This consideration should have special weight with preachers. Not a Christian thought exists which must go outside of the English tongue for a clear, precise, forcible utterance.

(5) Another reason for the scholarly conservation of our language in its purity is the fact that the knowledge and the use of it are rapidly extending over the nations of the world. English is clearly destined to be a living world-wide language for an incalculable period of time. Ministers should use their influence in preserving the purity of their language.

(6) The English language is in special danger of corruption in this country. We are made up from people of many nations and tongues. Dialects and provincialisms exist in many parts of our land. Slang finds easy acceptance among us.

(7) The clergy of a country have great influence over the tastes and usages of the people.

(8) The taste for purity of style is indispensable to thorough and refined scholarship.

6. *Since a pure style is of such importance to preachers of the Gospel, we must naturally inquire as to the most effective means of acquiring such a style.* We suggest four such means.

(1) Use pure English in habitual conversation. The conversation of the best class of educated men has an indefinable charm, due almost wholly to its selection of pure words, the predominance of Saxon words, the avoidance of slang, of contractions, of vulgarisms, of pedantic importations.

(2) Read the classic English authors. Delight in pure English. Let your tastes be formed upon the models of the English Bible, Shakespeare, Addison, Wordsworth, Macauley, Whately, Prescott, etc. Read with a caution those authors indifferent to the purity of their language.

(3) Use the dictionaries, grammars, and other treatises upon the language. Webster's dictionary is a nearly perfect authority for the signification of words.

(4) Practice scholarly care in your habits of composing. Never use a doubtful word without investigation. Generally

give preference to Saxon words. Criticize your own composition after the excitement of the work is over.

B. PRECISION

Precision is exactness. It is that quality by which a writer's style expresses no more, no less, and no other, than the thought which he means to express.

1. *Consider some of the ways precision can be violated*:

(1) One class of offenses against precision concerns the use or omission of single words, such as indefinite pronouns and connecting words.

(2) Another class of offenses concerns the literal and the figurative uses of the same words. Some words may be used literally and figuratively in the same sentence if care is not exercised.

(3) Precision of style are violated when synonyms are confounded. English style is rich in synonyms and critical discernment is especially needed to distinguish them.

(4) Precision may be violated not only by single words, but by the number of words. One can use too few words or too many words. Excessive conciseness and redundance both violate precision.

(5) Precision may be sacrificed further by looseness of construction.

2. *The chief causes of a loose style are these*:

(1) The habit of indiscriminate thinking. This is the first and chief cause. Let a speaker habitually think with

exactness, and a precise style will be at last inevitable. Some men are never precise writers or speakers bcause they never master anything to the full. They never get beyond the chaotic stage of culture.

(2) The indulgence of excessive care for expression as distinct from thought. High-sounding words are never to be substituted for more exact, plain words.

(3) Precision often suffers also from the want of a command of language. A genuine command of language is an acquisition, never a gift. An encouraging fact, at this point, is that the vocabulary which is necessary to effective speech is much less voluminous than is often supposed. Well educated people usually have a command of only a few thousand words.

(4) An uncritical admiration for loose writers will cause looseness of style.

(5) Another cause of looseness of style is a disproportioned amount of extemporaneous speech as compared with the products of the pen. Extemporizing promotes fluency of speech, but writing promotes precision.

Inducements to Cultivation of Precision

3. *Scarcely any other quality of speech has been made the object of so much impatient and sarcastic criticism as this of precision.* Men associate it with insipidity. In opposition to such an unscholarly attitude, let us note why we should cultivate precision.

(1) Precision does not necessitate in the result the acquisition of anything pedantic or unpractical. The ablest think-

ers are they who can put thought into its most exact expression.

(2) Precision and the study of it are essential to certain other qualities of good style. They assist clearness of style, energy of style, and elegance of style, and prevent an affected style.

(3) Precision is not only auxiliary to other qualities of a good style, but it has an independent virtue of its own. This is not easily defined, yet we all feel it. We respond approvingly to a precise style, not merely because it is clear, or vigorous, or becoming, but for its own sake. That is a keen mind which can say what it means, and all that it means; and we respect a keen mind.

(4) Precision of language is especially needed in many varieties of religious discourse. Much theological misunderstanding and controversy could be averted if meanings were expressed in exact definitions.

C. PERSPICUITY

Perspicuity of style is lucidity of style, transparency of thought. We need to consider this quality of style in reference to four things—thoughts, imagery, words, construction.

1. *Perspicuity must find its foundation in the thoughts to be expressed.* An important class of the causes of obscurity therefore, concerns the thoughts of the discourse.

(1) Obscurity may arise from the absence of thought. A man can not say what is not in him to say.

(2) Obscurity more often arises from vagueness of thought.

(3) Obscurity may spring also from the affectation of profound thought. When this disease of affected profoundness finds its way into the pulpit, it is the most offensive of all faults, if detected.

(4) Thought may give occasion for obscurity of style by its real profoundness. Subjects may be too abstruse for oral discussion. Simple truths may be pursued into complicated relations and handled abstrusely.

(5) A speaker's thought may lead him into an obscure style through his own familiarity with it. The very perfectness of a man's knowledge may impair his power to communicate.

(6) Thought may lead to obscure expression through rapidity in the succession of thoughts. The majority of minds require time to take in a difficult thought. A speaker may forget this fact and fail to illustrate and vary the form of statement because of his eageness to press on with his message.

2. *Perspicuity of style, having its foundation in the thoughts to be expressed, is further affected by the use of imagery.*

(1) Obscurity may arise from incongruous imagery. Imagery is painting, and the expressiveness of it is measured by its congruity.

(2) Similar is the obscurity caused by the use of mixed imagery. The mixture of metaphor with literal expression is often the cause of such obscurity.

(3) Obscurity may be occasioned by the employment of learned imagery. Jeremy Taylor made excessive use of im-

agery from the Greek classics and well-nigh ruined his style for practical uses.

(4) Another cause of obscurity in the use of imagery is an excess of imagery. This may obscure the meaning by exaggeration. Excess of imagery is particularly hurtful when no imagery is needed.

(5) Obscurity may be caused by the entire absence of imagery. Abstract thought needs to be made palatable by a proper use of imagery. The imaginative style in sermons needs to be cultivated, but should not be overdone.

3. *Perspicuity is related to the use of words in a discourse.*

(1) Obscurity will often result from the use of words which are more or less technical to religious usage.

(2) Obscurity may be induced by the preponderance in style of other than the Saxon elements of our language. The thinking and reading of the masses of the people are in Saxon dialect, hence they feel more at home with Saxon speech with any other.

(3) Perspicuity of style may very obviously be impaired by the habitual use of ambiguous words.

(4) Obscurity of style may be caused by an excessive use of general and abstract words. Oral discourse especially demands a specific and concrete vocabulary. Affectation in style may take the form of an evasion of concrete expression.

(5) Another occasion of obscurity in the use of language is an excessive diffuseness. Corpulent diction is ponderous and slow.

(6) On the other hand, there may be an excess of concise-ness. Conciseness is an aid to precision, but in excess impairs it.

4. *Perspicuity of style is vitally dependent on clearness of construction.* Construction is as vital to style as to architecture. Stiffness of obstruction tends to obscurity. Anything unfriendly to the sense of ease is inimical to clearness. Also monotony of construction, circumlocution in construction, and abruptness of construction tend to obscurity. We wish to indicate some of the specific ways in which obscurity may be due to construction.

(1) A defective arrangement of pronouns and their antecedents is one source of obscurity.

(2) A defective arrangement of adjectives and adverbs may also result in obscurity.

(3) A defective arrangement of the qualifying clauses of a sentence may bring about obscurity. The laws which govern qualifying clauses are the same as those which govern qualifying words, and the danger of obscurity is therefore the same.

(4) Another case of obscure construction may be a failure to express the true order of thought in the emphatic portions of a sentence.

(5) Obscure construction is often due to an excessive or careless use of ellipsis. Ellipsis refers to the omission of a word or words necessary to make the grammatical construction complete, which can be supplied from the context.

(6) A further cause of obscurity in construction is an abuse of the parenthesis. A parenthesis is a chasm, and the hearer must be able to vault over it. The length and the position of the parenthesis are determinative factors.

(7) Obscurity may also be caused by that figure of rhetoric which is technically termed "anacoluthon." This word means a lack of the usual grammatical coherence in a sentence, usually for special effect, as to express strong emotion. Few things are so fatal to the transparency of style as the adoption of the impassioned figures of speech when nothing in the thought demands them.

(8) Finally, rhetorical construction may be made obscure by the combination in one sentence of materials irrelevant to each other. Proximity of thoughts in one sentence implies mutual relationship. If none exists, that instinct of good hearing which expects it is balked. It looks for the point of connection and can find none.

D. ENERGY

Energy of style is difficult to define. It is not merely vivacity of style, nor the superlative of perspicuity, nor impressiveness of diction. We can only say that energy is a peculiar kind of impressiveness. It is the impressiveness of strength as distinct from that of clearness; the impressiveness of force as distinct from that of beauty; and the impressiveness of vigor as distinct from that of vivacity.

1. *The most important suggestions in the discussion of energy of style arrange themselves naturally under several topics* of which the first is the principle that the foundation

of a forcible discourse must be laid in the state of the writer's mind in the act of composing.

(1) A forcible writer must have thoughts to which forcible expression is appropriate. Unimportant thought, however clear, is not the proper subject of energy of expression; neither is indefiniteness of thought; nor is thought in which beauty or pathos is the predominant element.

(2) One should speak or write with enthusiasm to attain energy. The element of heat in all things prevents stagnation. Energy and enthusiasm co-exist in character and also in style.

(3) The materials to which energy of expression is apt, being in possession, energy requires still further, that, in the act of composing, the preacher shall write or speak with an immediate object in view. Finney never preached a sermon, or a fragment of one, without an object—a present object, an object made as luminous to the hearer as to the preacher, and an object which concerned the hearers more than all the world besides.

(4) Another element requisite to energy of style is that, in the act of composing, a preacher should be self-possessed. For superlative force in style a man must be master of his subject, his audience, his occasion. Enthusiasm also must be so under control as to be susceptible of use at the speaker's will.

How to Promote Energy

2. *Energy of style is assisted by certain means which are common to the literal and figurative use of language.*

(1) Energy is promoted by the use of pure words. Predominance should be given to Saxon words, specific words,

short words, and words whose sound is significant of their sense.

(2) Energy is regulated by the number of words. Conciseness is essential. Conciseness has been already considered as tributary to perspicuity and to precision, but it is more conducive to energy than to either. The most important violation of conciseness as affecting energy are tautology, verboseness, and needless circumlocution of thought.

(3) Not only does energy of style concern words considered singly; not only the number of words; but there is a class of tributaries to it which concerns the construction of sentences. In written composition especially three principles of rhetorical mechanism may be applied without detriment to freedom in composing.

(a) One is that emphatic words be so located that their force shall be obvious. This will usually be at the beginning or ending of a sentence.

(b) Energy may be expressed in the mechanical construction of style by the skillful use of the periodic structure. This is a construction in which the completion of the sense is suspended till the close.

(c) The periodic style assists energy of expression by a certain roundness of construction which is favorable to dignity of delivery.

3. *Energy of style is related to certain means which are peculiar to figurative speech.*

(1) The instinct of oratory numbers among its simplest figures of rhetoric the climax. Climactic order itself expresses

an idea, that of rise in thought. It is a symbol of culmination, and culmination of thought is force.

(2) The instinct of forcible utterance recognizes the energy of antithesis in style. Antithetic structure expresses the idea of contrast, and contrast itself is force.

(3) The interrogation is a tributary to energy of style. Few expedients of speech so simple as this are so effective in giving vigor to style. Interrogation invites response, expresses confidence in the hearers, and is an electric contact which carries from speaker to hearer the sign of vivid conviction.

(4) Hyperbole is a favorite figure of rhetoric among energetic writers. Hyperbole expresses strength of conviction in the preacher. It should not be overdone, or allowed to pass for reckless assertion.

(5) The forcibleness of irony needs no illustration, but does need to be used with caution.

(6) Exclamation deserves a caution rather than condemnation. It is excessively used in the pulpit.

(7) A speaker who is a perfect master of his imagination will sometimes instinctively choose the figure of vision to express his most powerful conceptions. The strictly prophetic state was a state of vision of the distant future. Yet note how instinctively secular oratory adopts the same expedient.

(8) The most passionate forms of eloquence employ the apostrophe with power. Some early Christian preachers used it to excess. The unseen world was very real to their faith, and therefore they often apostrophized the departed as if present to their eye. The soliloquy should properly be regarded as a variety of the apostrophe.

E. ELEGANCE

Elegance of style is the quality by which thought as expressed in language appeals to our sense of the beautiful. Beauty like strength is one of our ultimate conceptions. Beauty of style admits of partial analysis. Four distinct elements are discoverable in elegance. They are delicacy, vividness, variety, and harmony.

1. *Elegance of style then may be first considered as dependent on the element of delicacy.* It has its foundation in delicacy of thought. This might almost be called the feminine quality in thought. Woman originates certain conceptions more readily than man, and appreciates them more keenly. We must find the fundamental means of cultivating this quality in the cultivation of refinement of perception. The refined perception rejects that which is intrinsically coarse, or vulgar, or disproportioned. We can cultivate a refined perception by forming the habit of dwelling upon the beautiful in literature, art, and nature.

Elegance of style also demands delicacy of expression in the utterance of thought. Beauty of thought is more difficult to express than energy of thought. It requires a more sensitive discrimination of the significance of language. There are many offenses against elegance of style such as the bungling of dependent clauses, inelegance of imagery, the commonplace in imagery, unfinished imagery, and mongrel imagery. An elegant style demands a choice selection and arrangement of words.

2. *Elegance of style is dependent also on the element of vividness.* Vagueness if impression never produces beauty of impression. But beauty does not demand or admit of vividness in the superlative degree. The vividness which beauty demands must be such as shall consist with that delicacy which we have seen to be an equal element of beauty in discourse. Elegance of style as dependent upon vividness infers several things.

(1) Elegance demands distinctness of thought.

(2) From the necessity of vividness to beauty in speech, we infer further the necessity of sensitiveness of feeling to those varieties of eloquence in which the beautiful predominates. As energy of style demands force of feeling, elegance demands sensitiveness of feeling. Both are founded on the same principle.

(3) From the necessity of vividness to beauty we infer the value of original thought as the material of elegance in style. Thought which a writer or speaker feels to be his own, he will most readily express with sensitive emotion. Even the commonplaces of thought can be worked over to such a degree that the mind is quickened and refreshed to the equivalent of originality in expression.

(4) From the necessity of vividness as an element of beauty, we infer further, as a general fact, the necessity of simplicity of language to an elegant style. No other quality than beauty makes such an imperative demand for transparency.

(5) From the dependence of beauty on vividness of style, we infer the importance of an easy command of imagery to an elegant style. Write in pictures and you can not fail to

write vividly. Imagery is essential to vivid expression, especially because the vividness of beauty must be felt intuitively, not derived by reflective process.

3. *Our analysis of beauty leads us to consider elegance of style as dependent on variety.* In nature, music, and art this principle is demonstrated. Monotony, even of that which is in itself an excellence, destroys the beauty of any of these. The same is true of thought. One critic defines the whole art of composing as the art of varying thought skillfully. This raises the question, How may we acquire variety of style?

(1) Variety of style must have its foundation in versatility of thought. Thought in a versatile mind compels variety in its utterance. The preacher can use variety in method of discussion, variety of divisions in form and substance, variety in recapitulations of argument, and variety in applications— all these will help. As to cultivating mental versatility, read a versatile literature. Read other things than sermons. Write other things than sermons. Think and read much outside of professional channels. Keep out of mental ruts by an intellectual regimen which shall make the formation of such ruts impossible.

(2) That variety which elegance requires demands, also, a varied vocabulary and construction. The most essential requisite is a thorough command of the synonyms of the language, and the history of its literature. Avoid needless recurrence of the same word or same collocation of words, monotony in length of sentences, sameness in transitions, regularity of emphasis on beginning or end of sentences, etc.

(3) That variety which beauty of style requires involves variety of illustration. Draw illustrations from a multitude

of sources, and vary their length and type. And, for variety's sake, illustrations should not be restricted to any one rhetorical form, such as exclamation, apostrophe, or vision.

(4) The variety which an elegant taste requires is assisted by variety of delivery. A versatile delivery is not only the natural expression of a versatile style, but it is also a powerful auxiliary to the forming of such a style. Preachers must watch not to fall into a monotonous elocution, such as a nasal delivery, a drawling sing-sing delivery, a highly pitched delivery, or a weak drab delivery. A flexible voice, various intonation, gesture, and position, will aid the growth of a varied command of oral expression.

4. *Elegance is also dependent on the element of harmony.* Beauty is not only confined to objects which address the eye, but also to those which address the ear. Usage recognizes beauty in the structure of language. The element in language corresponding to proportion in form is what is meant by harmony. Harmony is influenced by several factors.

(1) The truthfulness of a discourse assists in disclosing its beauty to good taste. Truth may not of itself awaken the sense of beauty consciously; yet nothing susceptible of expression in language can be beautiful without it. Good taste acknowledges the direct effluence of truth as a thing of beauty.

(2) Unity of sentiment in a discourse assists the impression of beauty as discerned by good taste. Harmony is founded on oneness of aim in a well-constructed composition. There is a beauty of its own in symmetry of structure.

(3) Elegance is further promoted by the fitness of a discourse to the time, the place, the circumstances, and the characters concerned in its delivery. There is an elegance of propriety which depends chiefly on these considerations.

(4) Elegance, as dependent on harmony of style, is often assisted by euphonious language. A diction which flows easily, and therefore is pleasing to the ear, is becoming to the expression of beauty in thought. Euphony of style consists largely of three things—smoothness of vocabulary, melodious arrangement of clauses in the structure of sentences, and well-proportioned variety of structure in successive sentences. For cultivating a euphonious style we should give attention to the instinct of a good ear; give some deliberation and choice to diction in the act of composing; practice revision of style after composing, when the heat of the production has had time to cool; and break up distinctly metrical constructions.

F. NATURALNESS

Naturalness is that quality by which style expresses the fitness of language to thought, of both thought and language to the speaker, and of thought, language, and speaker to the hearer. It extends to all the fundamental elements out of which style grows. It stands related to them as proportion does to architecture. Primarily we do not reason about it, but we feel it, or we feel the absence of it. Since it is the resultant of qualities of style already discussed, the discussion of it as distinct from those must necessarily involve some repetition.

1. *Naturalness of style becomes perceptible to good taste in four forms.*

(1) Good taste approves naturalness of style in a certain fitness of expression to the subject of discourse. Style has a certain temper like that of steel which pervades every particle. A ponderous style is unsuited to some subjects, as is a volatile style unsuited to others.

(2) Naturalness of style becomes perceptible to good taste, also, in a certain fitness of thought and expression to the relations of hearers to the subject. Style must express truth to the range and quality of the conception of the hearers; otherwise, it is an unnatural style, as much so as if it expressed a falsehood.

(3) Naturalness of style becomes perceptible to good taste in a certain fitness of discourse to the relations of the speaker to his subject. That principle is violated by the dogmatic style, the patronizing style, the apologetic style, or the apathetic style. A natural style requires a just, temperate, manly appreciation, on the preacher's part, of his own personal relations to the truth he utters.

(4) Naturalness of style, again, becomes perceptible to good taste in a certain fitness of expression to oral discourse. The oral style of continuous discourse is distinct from that of the press on the one hand, and from that of conversation on the other. This distinction is hard to define, but has several features. They are the predominance of concrete over abstract words in its vocabulary; the inclination to a large excess of simplicity over intricacy in the construction of sentences; and the dramatic quality, which makes the hearer active in the discussion of a subject.

2. *By what means may a natural style be more effectually acquired?* The principal means are well known.

(1) The habit of mastering the subjects of discourse. Style depends more upon the permanent state of a writer's mind than upon any expedients of discipline, or moods of composition. Mastery is needed to create ease of movement. We do not write or speak naturally upon a subject which is not well mastered.

(2) Self-forgetfulness in the act of composing. Unnaturalness in almost any form of it may spring from an absence of composure. Self-consciousness in composure creates a strained style.

(3) An absorbing interest in the aim of a discourse. There is a difference between interest in the details of a discourse and interest in its aim. Always keep the practical object of a discourse in sight; keep it close at hand; let the shadow of it cover the whole structure from beginning to end. This unity of aim is itself natural and leads to naturalness of style.

(4) A strong confidence in the truth proclaimed. No man can preach well who has no faith. The loss of trust in truth may lead to the use of unnatural means of producing counterfeit results. Every preacher needs that calm and earnest trust in God's truth to do its appointed work in the lives of men which will make him what the world calls a natural orator.

(5) The final suggested means of acquiring a natural style is practice in composition. Usually the most prolific writer will be the most natural writer. The man who writes the largest quantity with critical care will write most naturally.

The state of prolific production, instead of degrading quality of output, elevates and enriches it.

This mental condition, in which composition becomes a delight, a necessity, a demand of nature upon a full mind, is the habit which a preacher needs to acquire in order to have uniform command of natural discourse. You can not acquire it but by large practice. Thinking and study alone will never give it. You must write and speak voluminously.

APPENDICES

Appendix I. *Men and Books* by Austin Phelps

Appendix II. Sermon Outlines by Austin Phelps

Appendix III. A Brief Biographical Sketch of Austin Phelps

Men and Books*

I propose in this book to speak of a preacher's *study of men* and of his *study of books* as sources of oratorical discipline.

I. The Independent Study of Men.

1. He should study himself and the processes of his own mind.

    (1) Every man's own experience reveals certain oratorical principles, such as what truths and speakers move his own mind, emotions, and will.

    (2) Every man's character is full of similar suggestions. What caused the greatest change in your character?

2. He should study other men.

    (1) Individual character in its rudest forms is power in speech.

    (2) The conduct of secular assemblies often discloses the working of power in speech.

    (3) Study masses of men under religious excitement.

3. This study of men is often undervalued because of a factitious reverence for books.

---

*This appendix is an outline of Dr. Austin Phelps' book, *Men and Books, or, Studies in Homiletics, Lectures Introductory to the Theory of Preaching*, Chas. Scribner's Sons, New York, 1882.

4. Enthusiasm in the study of men should be stimulated because of the popular idea that clergymen are ignorant of and separate from the world of men.

5. This defective idea of the clergyman as leading a routine, professional life, separated from the stern realities of common life, can be overcome.

6. Because of failure to study men, much preaching seems to apply to another world and not concern the practical affairs of this life.

7. The pulpit's ministry of comfort often fails because of lack of knowledge of men.

8. Watch the ministries of certain eccentric clergymen. They are not safe homiletic models, but they do furnish instructive hints to sounder men. They make men believe that preaching is a reality to them.

9. The literature of the world is not constructed for the masses of society. The pulpit is designed to reach all classes of people. The ministry of the pulpit must go beyond that of literature.

10. In the moral history of the world, great popular changes often take place independently of the educated classes of mankind as such. Clergymen should furnish Christian leadership for the masses.

11. The natural leaders of these movements of the popular mind, which are started by the first principles of religion, are the Christian ministry.

12. In every generation some clergymen oppose these popular movements which have their origin in Christian ideas. If they lived more among men, they would not do so.

13. When the pulpit ministers to the upper classes of society to the practical exclusion of the lower classes, it ceases to be a spiritual power with any class.

14. Any general deficiency in the clerical knowledge of the world must tend directly to obscure awareness of the biblical distinction between the regenerate and the unregenerate sections of society.

15. The study of living men as a source of discipline is commended by the general practice of leading minds in history.

II. The Study of Literature for Clerical Discipline.

1. The objects of the study of books. The general object is discipline as distinct from accumulation, but some more particular objects are:

   (1) A discovery of the principles of effective thought, and its expression in language;

   (2) That familiarity with the principles of effective thought and expression which gives one a working knowledge of those principles as distinct from a critical knowledge;

   (3) Assimilation to the genius of the best authors;

   (4) To facilitate a man's knowledge of his own powers and adaptations to professional labor.

   The selection of authors for pastoral study.

   (1) Put out of our account of literature vicious and worthless books.

   (2) We must abandon the idea of universal scholarship. The idea of literary omniscience long ago became a fable.

(3) We should rank first in our estimate those authors who have been controlling powers in literature. They are not numerous. The perpetuity of their influence should give them first rank with us. We must often sacrifice time from some good literature in order to give time to the best.

(4) In our choice of authors, the literature of the English language should predominate. The English literature is intrinsically superior to any other.

(5) The just claims of American literature should be recognized.

(6) The true idea of a pastor's reading must be regulated in part by his professional duties. He must do considerable reading for direct homiletical purposes.

(7) Our choice of authors should cover as large a range of literature as can be read in a scholarly way. A certain variety of knowledge is necessary to the perfection of any one species of knowledge. Ministers are under peculiar temptations to narrow discipline.

(8) A scholarly ideal of study includes the study of unwritten literature. I refer to the utterances of the living voice, great orations, powerful sermons, masterly debates, and even everyday conversations. A study of printed literature alone may give us a false conception of what oral eloquence is.

(9) We should study the Scriptures as literary classics. Biblical literary models are intrinsically superior to all others. Furthermore, living literature is deeply

indebted to the Bible—as much as vegetation is indebted to light.

III. Methods of Literary Study.

1. The ideal of scholarly reading is critical reading.

2. Scholarly reading is reading in the spirit of philosophical inquiry.

3. The most useful reading is done by a scholarly division of labor. Critical attention should be directed to one thing at a time. Deep boring can be done only in spots.

4. The scholarly ideal of reading involves studious comparison of authors with each other.

5. As far as possible, our reading should be made tributary to the correction of our own known deficiencies in literary production.

6. A scholarly ideal of reading includes a study of the biographies of authors and the history of their times. A book is part of an author's life. We need to see it as part of the man.

7. A preacher's study of literature should be accompanied with habitual practice in composition. A pastor's compulsory habits of production are rather a help than a hindrance to the scholarly character of his reading. I recommend commencing each day with an hour or more of studious reading, and then pass, without interval, to the work of composing. This practice is followed by many eminent authors.

8. In our studies, a generous appreciation of the genius of others should be balanced by a just estimate of our own. Neither is healthy without the other.

IV. The Practicability of Literary Study to a Pastor.

1. Let us first note some preliminary suggestions.

   (1) Any plan of study will usually be to a greater or less extent an ideal one. However, even though you may not read all you plan, you will read something.

   (2) The study of books need not be made impracticable by the study of men. Pastoral work gives large opportunity for the study of men without detracting from the study of books.

   (3) Some plan of reading must be made practicable if a pastor would save himself from intellectual decline.

   (4) The best culture for success in the pastoral office must not be subordinated to administrative and executive work both inside and outside the parish.

   (5) Any plan of clerical study will fail which is not founded upon a stern physical discipline.

   (6) Any plan has little probability of success which is not assisted by certain moral virtues. You can not work well with your brains and your heart in conscious conflict.

   (7) No plan will probably succeed which is not in some important features your own. Scarcely any two men can execute well the same plan of scholarly study.

(8) No plan will be likely to succeed which is founded upon a scholastic ideal alone. Yours must be a professional mind, scholarly, yet not scholastic.

(9) Form your plan of study so as to secure as much concentration of effort as is practicable.

(10) You should so form your plan of study that it can sustain interruptions. A pastor's plans are subject to frequent interruptions.

(11) Your courage in pursuing any plan you may devise should be sustained by the certainty of your mental growth.

2. A plan of pastoral study in English literature.

(1) Run a line of professional reading through the history of the literature.

(2) Pursue collateral lines of reading as they are suggested by professional studies. By the law of literary association, collateral lines of reading will branch out in all directions.

(3) Portions of our literature which are remotely connected with the pulpit should be read by departments. Read continuously for a while by departments, instead of reading fragmentarily here and there.

(4) Generally plan to occupy fragments of time with standard literature. Fragments of time must be utilized or the loss in the aggregate is immense.

(5) Much of the light literature of the language may be naturally reserved for periods of relief from professional labor.

(6) I would suggest reading the works of the most eminent of English and American preachers in historic clusters, associating these clerical names with their secular contemporaries. I give only the names of the preachers. They are John Wickliffe, William Tyndale, John Knox, Hugh Latimer, Thomas Cranmer, Richard Hooker, Archbishop Leighton, Jeremy Taylor, Isaac Barrow, Robert South, Richard Baxter, John Bunyan, Stephen Charnock, John Howe, Samuel Clark, Ralph Erskine, Bishop Butler, Hugh Blair, William Paley, John Wesley, George Whitefield, Samuel Hopkins, Robert Hall, John Foster, Thomas Chalmers, Timothy Dwight, Nathaniel Emmons, Jonathan Edwards, William E. Channing, Edward Pusey, Archbishop Whately, Frederick Robertson, Albert Barnes, Horace Bushnell, Chas. G. Finney, and Francis Wayland.

APPENDIX II

Sermon Outlines

by Austin Phelps*

A TOPICAL OUTLINE

What Do We Know of the Heavenly Life?

Introduction:

1. Thousands of aged and ill Christians live along the border-line between two worlds.

2. They particularly wish to know about conditions in the next life.

3. Much about that life we cannot know.

Proposition: 4. Some things about the heavenly life we do know, not with the knowledge of demonstration, but by the testimony of revelation, or by the proof of strong natural probability.

Transitional, or key, sentence: Note some facts about the heavenly life that we do know.

---

*These outlines have been lifted out of the written messages of Dr. Phelps. This first one is taken from *My Portfolio, a Collection of Essays*, by Austin Phelps, Chas. Scribner's Sons, New York, 1882, chap. 31.

I. **An Emancipation from a Dying, and in its Best State, a Restrictive Body.**

1. Emancipation from death.

2. Emancipation from the restrictions of sense.

II. **An Enlarged Range and an Augmented Intensity of Mental Powers.**

1. A deeper insight into truth.

2. An abounding overflow of mental capacities.

III. **The Soul's Natural Dominion Over Material Things Grandly Developed.**

1. Mind will probably be independent of the veto of matter.

2. Movement with the speed of thought is likely.

IV. **An Intensified Consciousness of Personal Identity.**

1. We will know ourselves and our friends.

2. The Bible indicates an intensified individuality.

3. Memory and conscience will be more efficient there than here.

V. **A New Sense of the Personality, the Perfections, and the Friendship of God.**

1. Through new affinities with God's character.

2. Through moral sympathy with God.

3. Through removal from Satanic deceptions.

VI. A Life of Happy Occupations.

1. Joyful worship.

2. Untiring and dignified service.

Conclusion:

1. We see heaven to be an inviting place.

2. We see that faithful Christians will not be disappointed.

3. Does our present character fit in well with heaven's pure and lofty attractions?

AN INFERENTIAL SERMON OUTLINE*
Presumption in the Worship of God

Text: 2 Chron. 26:16-20 (concerning Uzziah being smitten with leprosy for intruding into the priest's office).

Introduction:

1. The punishment of sin by bodily disease is usually long in coming.

2. Uzziah's case is one of the few Biblical instances of instant and severe punishment for irreverence and presumption.

3. That irreverent worshipers are not all lepers is no proof that they are more pleasing to God than Uzziah.

Proposition and key sentence: 4. Let us note some of the ways in which the guilt of presumption in the worship of God is often incurred in modern times.

---

*Taken from *Studies of the Old Testament* by Austin Phelps, Congregational Publishing Society, Boston, 1879, pp. 79-88.

I. Sleeping in God's House.

1. The infirm and diseased may be excusable.
2. No excuse for the strong and well.
3. Few things of the silent sort can be more impertinent to the most high God.

II. Neglecting to Participate in Divine Worship When Present in God's House.

1. Negative sins are often most intensely sinful.
2. Being in the atmosphere of worship, prayer, and praise, without participating, deadens the conscience.
3. Spiritual ossification is a slow but deadly disease.

III. Frequenting the House of God as a Place of Entertainment Merely.

1. Entertainment aspect of some church services supersedes the worship aspect.
2. Jesus strongly condemned using the Temple for gain instead of for prayer.
3. Would Jesus use the whip of cords if He came to some churches today?

IV. Endeavoring to Conceal from Ourselves Hidden Sin Under Cover of Scrupulous Devotion.

1. Micah, of the time of the Judges, with his private idol and priest, is an example.
2. Men can persuade themselves that religious devotions can offset crimes.
3. How idiotic we become when we make Satan our ally!

V. Offering to God Services in Which Any Essential Truth of God's Being Is Denied or Ignored.

1. Denying the Trinity.

2. Stripping Christ of some of His deity.

3. Praying in some other name than that of Jesus.

Conclusion: No final conclusion given.

AN EXPOSITORY SERMON OUTLINE*
An Ancient Revival of Religion

Text: 2 Chron. 15:8-15 (concerning the revival in Judah under King Asa).

Introduction:

1. Some claim that revivals are of modern origin.

Proposition: 2. But here is a revival which tallies with singular accuracy with similar works of divine grace in our own day.

3. Discussion of the setting and course of Asa's revival.

4. This is a clear case of deliberate seeking for and working for a revival of religion, and with success.

Transitional sentence: 5. Consider the permanent revival principles demonstrated here.

————

*ibid., pp. 43-54.

I. The Heart of a Revival Lies in a Renewal of the Covenant of the Church With God,

Vs. 15:12, "They entered into a covenant to seek the Lord God of their fathers, with all their heart and with all their soul." Vs. 15:15, "And all Judah rejoiced at the oath; for they had sworn with all their heart, and sought him with their whole desire."

1. A revival begins in the church of Christ.

2. The people must be dead in earnest.

II. A Public Proclamation of a Revived Faith Before the World,

Vs. 15:14, "And they sware unto the Lord in a loud voice, and with shouting, and with trumpets, and with cornets."

1. They made great ado about the regeneration of the realm.

2. Men must proclaim God's deliverance to those who need the same.

III. It Was Attended with a Great Influx of Converts from Without,

Vs. 15:9, ". . . the strangers . , , fell to him out of Israel in abundance, when they saw that the Lord his God was with him."

1. The heart of the world responds to the heart of the church.

2. A feeling of awe becomes general in a community in which the Holy Spirit is moving with great power.

IV. A Thorough Reformation of Public and Private Morals,

Vs. 15:8, "Asa . . , took courage and put away the abominable idols out of the land."

1. True revival changes life privately and publicly.

2. Anything less is cant and hypocrisy.

V. Often Such Awakenings Are Followed by Periods of Temporal Prosperity,

Vs. 15:15, ". . . and the Lord gave them rest round about."

1. The symbol of all temporal blessings is a state of peace.

2. All the facts bear witness that the drift of religious living is to better man's worldly condition.

Conclusion: No separate conclusion given.

A TEXTUAL-TOPICAL SERMON OUTLINE*

An Ancient Model of Youthful Temperance

Text:

Daniel 1:8, "But Daniel purposed in his heart that he would not defile himself with the portion of the king's meat, nor with the wine which he drank."

Introduction:

1. The Old Testament often seems as if it were inspired especially for young men.

---

*ibid., pp. 174-186. I have been unable to find a truly textual sermon among Dr. Phelps' writings.

2. Our lesson answers the question, What stand shall I take respecting obedience to the drinking usages of society?

3. Daniel was a young prophet, and comes home to every young man's level.

Proposition. 4. Let us listen and overhear the young prophet's counsel as to drinking, by asking and answering three questions.

I. What Were Daniel's Temptations to Abandon a Life of Abstinence from Strong Drink?

1. He was tempted by his youth.

2. He was tempted by the usages of his social rank.

3. He was tempted by the courtesies of official station.

4. He was tempted by his professional prospects.

5. He was tempted by his absence from home and native land.

II. What Was the Young Nobleman's Conduct in the Trial?

1. He was true to his faith in abstinence from the use of wine.

2. He was true to the education of his childhood.

3. He was true to the principle of temperance as a religious virtue.

4. He calmly trusted the consequences of his procedure to God.

III. What Were the Results of Daniel's Fidelity in His Own Experience?

1. By his temperance he gained a healthy body.

2. By his temperance he gained an unsullied conscience.

3. By his temperance he laid the foundation of a robust, religious manhood.

4. By his temperance he settled the future of his professional career as a prophet of the living God.

Conclusion:

1. Daniel is destined to live forever in the grateful and reverent affections of mankind, while the monarchs of his day are remembered only because of Daniel.

2. The foundations of this destiny were laid far back in his youth.

3. Let this friend of temperance and child of conscience inspire and guide us.

These outlines by Dr. Phelps reveal the differences between the core-word, or idea, and the key-word. The core-idea carries the subject down through the introduction, proposition, and main divisions, into the conclusion. The key-word is the principle of division suggested by the proposition or the transitional sentence. All main divisions should fall easily into the category suggested by the key-word.

In the first outline (topical) the key-word is "facts" and comes in the transitional sentence. Each main division is a "fact" regarding the heavenly life. The core-idea is "the heavenly life" and is either stated or inferred down through the whole outline.

The second outline represents an inferential sermon. The key-word in the proposition is "ways," and every main division is a "way" people may be guilty of presumption in worship. The core-idea is "presumption in worship" and is implied throughout the outline. This phrase could well be added to each main division to complete its meaning.

In the third outline (expository) the key-word in the proposition is "principles" and every main division is a revival principle. The core-idea is "revival" and is stated or suggested in each part of the outline.

The fourth outline (textual-topical) gives the key-word "questions" in the proposition. Each main division is a question and the subdivisions answer the question. The core-idea is "temperance" or "abstinence" and binds the whole outline together. It is either stated or inferred in each main section of the sermon.

An Outline by the Reviser

Subject: **GLORIFYING GOD**

Scripture: Acts 6:3—8:2

Introduction:

1. The highest function of life is to glorify God.

2. All creation below man glorifies God, Psalm 19:1, 29:9.

3. Jesus made it his supreme life purpose to glorify God, John 12:28, 17:1, 5, 10, 22, 24. Define glorifying God.

Proposition:

4. Stephen's life illustrates three ways by which we can glorify God.

Divisions:

I. HE GLORIFIED GOD IN HIS CHARACTER, Acts 6:3, 5, 8

1. He was a man of good report, 6:3
2. He was full of the Holy Spirit and wisdom, 6:3
3. He was a man of faith, 6:5
4. He was full of grace and power, 6:8
5. He accepted responsibility, 6:3

II. HE GLORIFIED GOD IN HIS TESTIMONY, 6:8—8:2

1. He testified with power, 6:10
2. He testified in many places, 6:8-9
3. He testified boldly, 6:11—7:53
4. He testified to the Scriptures, 7:2-50
5. He testified effectively, 7:54
6. He testified to a heavenly vision, 7:55-56

III. HE GLORIFIED GOD IN HIS DEATH, 7:57—8:2

1. He died in active service, 7:57-58
2. He died praying, 7:60
3. He died triumphantly, 7:55-56
4. He died deeply mourned, 8:2
5. He died impressing Saul with Christianity's power, 8:1

Conclusion:

1. Since Stephen was not an Apostle but a layman, his example is an encouragement to all of us.

2. Let us fulfill the supreme function of life as Stephen did.

———

This outline exemplifies several homiletical principles. It is a topical expository sermon. The core-idea runs through the whole outline—glorifying God. Note this idea in the subject, introduction, proposition, main divisions, and the conclusion. The proposition infolds the outline. The outline develops the proposition. The key-word in the proposition is "ways." Each main division is a "way" to glorify God. All subdivisions unfold the main division under which they fall. All main divisions are mutually exclusive, yet related. These main divisions are in parallel construction. Every point has Scriptural support.

APPENDIX III

Biographical Sketch of Austin Phelps *

Austin Phelps was born January 7, 1820, in Brookfield, Mass., in the parsonage of the Orthodox Congregational Church, where his father had been the pastor about four years. He received a careful Christian training in the home. He was a precocious child, being able to read the Bible at family prayers when only four years old, and able to do any sum in cube root at the age of eight. He was prepared for college when he was twelve, but did not enter until the following year. He went to Hobart College, Geneva, N. Y., for almost two years, then was transferred by his father to Amherst College. When within a month of graduation from Amherst the family moved to Philadelphia, and young Austin Phelps was transferred to the University of Pennsylvania. At this period in his life two men greatly influenced him. They were Professor Henry Reed, head of the English department at the University, who instilled into him a passion for good literature and excellence of English style; while the other man was Dr. Albert Barnes, a Presbyterian pastor, whose powerful orthodox preaching and personal friendship mightily stimulated the youthful student to higher and better things.

Dr. Phelps does not point to any time in his life when he experienced conversion to God. He was under strong religious

*This sketch is based on the book, *Austin Phelps, a Memoir*, by Elizabeth Stuart Phelps, a daughter, Scribner's, N. Y., 1891.

influences all his life and never thought of himself otherwise than as a Christian. He did pass through a powerful revival in his twelfth year, when he attended many children's prayer-meetings, prayed much, and thought of little else than the salvation of his own soul. He could well remember hearing Charles G. Finney preach at that time. Under the preaching of Dr. Albert Barnes he made a profession of religion at the age of eighteen, but in spite of the fact that he diligently sought the Jonathan Edwards and Charles G. Finney type of conversion, he had no emotional experiences at all.

Austin Phelps graduated from the University of Pennsylvania in 1837, at the age of 17. He began seminary work at the New York Seminary, but in 1839, went to the New Haven Seminary. He was licensed to preach by the Third Presbytery of Philadelphia in 1840. He accepted a call to the Pine Street Presbyterian Church, Boston, in April, 1842. The same year in September he married Elizabeth Stuart, the eldest daughter of Professor Moses Stuart, the distinguished biblical scholar of Andover Theological Seminary. He was soon recognized as an outstanding preacher, and received calls to other churches and to professorships in theological seminaries. After only six years in his first pastorate, at the age of twenty-six, he accepted the call to take the chair of homiletics at Andover Theological Seminary.

He gave himself to his new task with utmost energy and faithfulness. His lecture room became the altar of his life. He allowed nothing to blaspheme it. He carefully rewrote his lectures every year. He was patient and considerate, yet exacting and thorough with his students. He loved his students and was loved by them. His lectures were wise, scholarly, conscientious, and exhaustive discussions. They seemed to glow with the heat of recent thinking. He set a remarkable example of the refined and cultured Christian scholar, the modest and dignified gentleman, the beloved teacher, critic, counsellor and friend. He was relentless in urging his students on to the highest standards of homiletic excellence.

Dr. Phelps was a pulpit orator and a spiritual orator. He was a magnetic preacher. In appearance, he was of average height, well-proportioned, with a fine head, a broad full brow, flashing blue eyes, and thin sensitive lips. When preaching, "the whole vividness of the man poured itself along his words like molten gold. He seemed to be eaten up by his theme. It ran through him like a fever. Yet his self-possession was perfect... His manner was essentially quiet, controlled and finished. The fire burned through; that was all. One felt his emotion more because of what he so evidently restrained than because of what he expressed. . . . But probably the most powerful element in his pulpit manner was his voice. This cannot be described, but is not soon forgotten. Low, distinct, and vibrating, it rose to rebuke, or fell to awe, or melted to tenderness; it throbbed through the hearer like the nerves of a soul."* His preaching was characterized by elegance of diction, fineness of form, power of address, and intensity of spiritual passion.

His wife, Elizabeth Stuart, died Nov. 29, 1852, three months after the birth of their third child. In April, 1854, he married the sister of his wife, Mary Stuart. She already had the tuberculosis and did not live long, but he married her because he wished to take care of her. In June, 1858, he married Mary A. Johnson of Boston. This union lasted thirty-three years and gave him much happiness. His two younger sons were born from this marriage.

Austin Phelps, by Elizabeth Stuart Phelps, Scribner's, N. Y., 1891, pp. 105-106.

Professor Phelps did not have vigorous health. Soon after becoming a professor at Andover, his eyes failed, and he labored under this handicap many years. Because of poor health he finally withdrew from active service at Andover in 1879, and became professor emeritus. He battled illness and failing strength to the end of his days, which came October 13, 1890. He was buried in the churchyard of Andover chapel beside his first wife.

While his last eleven years of life were marked by bad health, yet this was the productive literary period of his life. He spent the summers of his last twenty years at Bar Harbor, Maine, and seemed to suffer less there than anywhere else. He is the author of the following books:

> The Still Hour
> The Solitude of Christ
> The Sabbath Hymn Book
> > (with Professor Park and Dr. Mason)
> Sabbath Hours
> The New Birth
> The Theory of Preaching
> Men and Books
> English Style in Public Discourse
> Old Testament Studies
> My Portfolio
> My Study
> My Note-Book

His most widely circulated book was *The Still Hour,* a small devotional classic on prayer. Austin Phelps was a man of prayer, a preacher of power, and a peerless teacher of preaching.